Robert Dudley Baxter

The Taxation of the United Kingdom

Robert Dudley Baxter

The Taxation of the United Kingdom

ISBN/EAN: 9783742813893

Manufactured in Europe, USA, Canada, Australia, Japa

Cover: Foto ©knipser5 / pixelio.de

Manufactured and distributed by brebook publishing software (www.brebook.com)

Robert Dudley Baxter

The Taxation of the United Kingdom

THE TAXATION

OF THE

UNITED KINGDOM.

BY

R^t DUDLEY BAXTER, M.A.

PARTLY READ BEFORE THE STATISTICAL SOCIETY OF
LONDON, JANUARY 19, 1869.

"Follow Facts."

London:
MACMILLAN AND CO.
1869.

[The Right of Translation is reserved.]

BY THE SAME AUTHOR.

8vo. 100 pp. price 3s. 6d.

NATIONAL INCOME.

THE UNITED KINGDOM.

Read before the Statistical Society of London, January 21, 1868.

LONDON: MACMILLAN & CO.
1868.

PREFACE.

THE First Part of the following work, with a short sketch of two Chapters of the Second Part, was read, in January last, before the Statistical Society of London, and had the advantage of the suggestions of its Members, and the criticisms of the Press.

The Second Part, which now constitutes the main portion of the work, is almost entirely new, and embraces the important questions of Rating, of the relative Taxation of Land, Personalty, and Industry, and of the indirect effect of Taxes upon Prices.

On all the subjects discussed, the greatest pains have been taken to obtain accurate information, and from the most reliable sources. The public Statistics have been drawn from Parliamentary Returns, and from the works of Porter and

McCulloch; and most valuable assistance has been kindly given by Mr. Gripper, the Controller General of the Inland Revenue Department.

The circumstances of the different Trades in taxable articles have been supplied by very eminent wholesale and retail firms in each department, and checked by numerous inquiries among the smaller retail dealers.

The Consumption of taxable commodities by the different Classes of the community has been ascertained by diligent inquiry, as well as by Returns furnished by correspondents in many different parts of the country, in which I have had the hearty co-operation of gentlemen on both sides of politics. A suggestion made by Mr. Wentworth Dilke, M.P., has been adopted, of obtaining actual examples of the expenditure of Working Men both in London, in Town, and in Country, so as to contrast their habits and taxation.

I trust that the body of facts thus collected may be of permanent value as a record of the past progress and present condition of the population of the United Kingdom, independently of the transitory circumstances of its present Taxation.

Of the deductions from these facts, I can only say that they have been made "without fear, favour, or affection," and with no object but that of ascertaining and explaining the truth, in whatever direction it may lead. The conclusions, in particular, respecting the Rating Question, and the comparative Taxation of Land, Personalty, and Industry, are different from those which, in common with the great majority of the reading public, I had held on these subjects, and in the latter instance are against my own predilections and interest as the possessor of an Industrial Income.

In so large and untrodden a field of inquiry—in which this little work may almost be said to be a pioneer—I cannot hope to have escaped all error. But I trust that the facts to which it calls attention, and the investigations which it may occasion, will promote a more systematic and scientific revision, and improvement, of the Taxation of the United Kingdom; and so be conducive to the permanent welfare and prosperity of the Nation.

HAMPSTEAD,
March 24th, 1869.

CONTENTS.

PART I.—AMOUNT OF TAXATION.

CHAP.		PAGE
I.	THE RESOURCES AND EXPENDITURE OF THE UNITED KINGDOM	7
II.	THE PRINCIPLES OF TAXATION	11
III.	THE MODES OF TAXATION	15
IV.	THE NOMINAL AND ACTUAL TAXATION OF THE UNITED KINGDOM	23
V.	TAXES ON INCOME AND PROPERTY	26
VI.	TAXES ON EXPENDITURE	30
VII.	TAXES ON TRADES, PROFESSIONS, AND INTERCOURSE	34
VIII.	LOCAL RATES AND TOLLS	37
IX.	SUMMARY OF TAXATION	40

PART II.—DISTRIBUTION AND PRESSURE OF TAXATION.

X.	THE PRESSURE OF TAXATION	45
XI.	TAXES ON PROPERTY DO NOT BECOME RENT CHARGES	50
XII.	THE RATING QUESTION	59
XIII.	THE CONSUMPTION OF CORN, TEA, COFFEE AND SUGAR	68
XIV.	THE CONSUMPTION OF TOBACCO AND ALCOHOL	79
XV.	TAXES ON PROPERTY AND INCOME	92
XVI.	TAXES ON TRADES AND PROFESSIONS, AND CONVEYANCE	101
XVII.	TAXES ON EXPENDITURE	105
XVIII.	COMPARATIVE TOTAL TAXATION	115
XIX.	LAND, PERSONALTY, AND INDUSTRY	123
XX.	THE EXTRA COST OF TAXES	128
XXI.	SUMMARY AND CONCLUSION	142

APPENDICES.

I.	PROPERTY OF THE UNITED KINGDOM		163
II.	UPPER AND MIDDLE CLASSES.		
	1. ESTABLISHMENTS AND CONSUMPTION		165
	2. CONSUMPTION OF WINES AND SPIRITS		166
III.	TAXATION OF THE MANUAL LABOUR CLASSES		167
IV.	COMPARATIVE TOTAL TAXATION OF THE UPPER AND MIDDLE AND WORKING CLASSES		174
V.	VALUE OF TEA, COFFEE, AND SUGAR, AND OF WINE, BEER, AND SPIRITS		177

INTRODUCTION.

If, at the commencement of some happy era, a wise and perfect House of Commons—elected without bribery or treating, intimidation or rioting, by universal suffrage of every person of education and intelligence—were to propose to her Majesty the revision of our Taxation, in order to bring it into accordance with the soundest and most enlightened principles of political economy, the first step would naturally be to institute a public inquiry into the merits and practical effects of the existing fiscal system. The most experienced servants of the Crown would be called on for their evidence, and the official Returns ransacked for information as to the working of each Tax, to ascertain whether it was equitable and free from oppression, whether it interfered as little as possible with commerce, and whether its collection was easy and inexpensive. But when the principle and operation of every impost had been examined, and the most faultless modes of taxation discovered, one series of questions would still remain—the most important of the whole investigation—How much, under any given system, will each man pay? Whether rich, or whether poor, will every one pay his fair and equitable proportion, neither more nor less, of the burdens of the State? Will every class and individual, of whatever income, be assessed on a scale of perfect justice?

Such an inquiry, with the public evidence which it produced, and the legislative measures by which it would be followed, might be of inestimable value to the Commonwealth. It would bring about the removal of inequalities and injustices of Taxation, wherever they could be shown to exist. It would improve the condition of the people by taking away every hindrance to their welfare and progress. It would convince the poor that they were treated with complete fairness, and that the burdens they were called upon to bear were the least that could be demanded by the justice of the State.

But before those golden days arrive, and without waiting for Parliamentary authority or official omniscience, it may be useful for us, so far as our means of information allow, to attempt a similar investigation respecting the existing system of Taxation, and to lay the collected facts before this

Society, as forming one of the Committees of that great Parliament of scientific inquirers who so often prepare the way for future legislation.

Such an investigation will be of private as well as public interest. We all pay Taxes, but scarcely one of us knows how much he pays, and how the money is taken. Indirect taxation is like bloodletting, where the patient is kept in ignorance of the quantity abstracted. Let us try to fathom some of the secrets of Taxation, and each ascertain our own share of the burden.

PART I.

Amount of Taxation.

CHAPTER I.

THE RESOURCES AND EXPENDITURE OF THE UNITED KINGDOM.

LET us first consider the resources and territories of the United Kingdom. Two small islands, with a total area of 120,000 square miles, mere specks in the ocean compared with the vast regions of the habitable globe, have become, by the energy and good fortune of their inhabitants, the most wealthy and influential country of the earth. *Comparative smallness of the United Kingdom.*

By 250 years of colonization and conquest we have filled with our fellow-subjects or subjected to our sway large territories in Canada, the West Indies, Asia, Africa, and Australasia, with a total area of four and a half millions of square miles, and 155,000,000 of population. *Our Colonies and Conquests.*

By 100 years of mechanical invention and manufacturing industry—during which we originated and brought into general use the two greatest agents of *Our Manufactures and Commerce.*

modern civilization, the Steam-engine and the Railway—we have developed a commerce which covers the sea with ships, carrying to and from every quarter of the globe a total value of £500,000,000 of exports and imports.

Our dense Population.
Our population, under the stimulus of this vast employment, has grown to be the densest of the great European nations, and now numbers more than thirty millions, greater by one fourth than our agriculture can support.

Our gross Income.
See "National Income," p. 64.
Our Income has increased by rapid strides, through the growth of profitable and highly-paid industries, to a gross total of £800,000,000 per annum, of which £325,000,000 is derived from the weekly wages of the Manual Labour Classes.

Our Property and Capital.
See Appendix I.
Property has accumulated in the hands of a comparatively small number of landed proprietors and capitalists, to an estimated total of £6,000,000,000 of land and personalty.

National Debt.
We are burdened with a public Debt, which (including the £50,000,000 Capital of the Terminable Annuities) amounts in the whole to nearly £800,000,000, and involves an annual taxation for interest of £26,600,000, or $3\frac{1}{3}$ per cent. on our gross Income.

Army and Navy.
We maintain, for the national defence and for the garrisons of our Colonies and possessions, an Army,

which, in 1867-8, cost £15,400,000 ; and for the protection of our coasts and commerce a Navy, costing £11,200,000 ; amounting together to £26,600,000, or another 3⅓ per cent. on our gross Income. *Chap. I.*

We carry on the government and internal administration of the country by a Civil Service, a Diplomatic Corps, Courts of Justice, a Postal Service, Educational Grants, and Collectors of the Revenue, at a cost of £16,000,000, or 2 per cent. on our gross Income. *Internal administration.*

We support the destitute Poor, keep up the Police and Highways, pave, light, and sewer our towns and cities, and maintain Harbours, Bridges, and Markets, by a local taxation estimated at £22,500,000, or nearly 3 per cent. on our gross Income. *Local Taxation.*

Such are the four great heads of our expenditure, amounting together to £91,500,000, or 11½ per cent. on our gross Income.

The following table gives more briefly the figures which have just been recapitulated :—

RESOURCES, EXPENDITURE, AND EMPIRE OF THE UNITED KINGDOM, 1868. *Summary.*

AREA in square miles .	120,000
POPULATION . .	30,000,000
GROSS INCOME . .	£800,000,000
GROSS PROPERTY	£6,000,000,000
NATIONAL DEBT .	£800,000,000

10   The Resources of the United Kingdom.

Per centage on Gross Income.		EXPENDITURE (including Collection and Management):—		
3⅛	(1)	Interest on Debt	£26,600,000	
3½	(2)	{ Army £15,400,000 { Navy £11,200,000	£26,600,000	
2	(3)	Civil Administration	£16,000,000	
2⅝	(4)	Poor and Local	£22,500,000	
11½				£91,500,000

COMMERCE:—
Imports	£275,000,000	
Exports	£225,000,000	
		£500,000,000

COLONIAL EMPIRE —
Area (square miles)	4,500,000
Population	155,000,000

Conclusions. These figures are enormous, and show clearly the foundations upon which our prosperity is based. The United Kingdom is so populous and wealthy, because she is the metropolis of a vast empire, and the centre of a vast commerce. Our existence as a wealthy nation depends upon our pre-eminence. Whatever may be the cost of maintaining that pre-eminence, it must be cheerfully paid, as the truest national economy.

But expenditure need not be wasteful. A commercial people, who depend for their market upon the cheapness of their production, can afford no waste. Efficiency and economy should be the maxim of their Government.

CHAPTER II.

THE PRINCIPLES OF TAXATION.

"EQUALITY of Taxation" is the maxim which, since the days of Adam Smith, has been recognised by the great majority of thinking men, but there has been much controversy as to the manner in which it should be carried into practice. Adam Smith and the earlier economists maintained that it should mean *contribution in proportion to income*. He says :— Chap. II. Equal Taxation. Adam Smith.

> "The subjects of every State ought to contribute towards the support of the Government as nearly as possible in proportion to their several abilities; that is, *in proportion to the revenue which they respectively enjoy under the protection of the State.*" Book V. chap. ii. part 2.

So that the rich man and the poor should each be assessed at an equal *per centage* on his annual incomings.

For instance, in England, where (as will be shown) the actual taxation amounts to 10 per cent. on income, Adam Smith's rule would tax in the following proportions:—

	£
A Wealthy Man with £5,000 a-year . . .	500
A Professional Man or Tradesman with £500 a-year	50
A Working Man with £50 a-year	5

Bentham and Mill.

But Bentham and Mill and the later economists have urged with much reason that this is not true equality, since the poor man's payment out of the necessaries of life is a far greater sacrifice than a rich man's payment out of comforts or luxuries. They maintain, and the opinion has been generally accepted, that the poor man ought to be lightly taxed, or altogether exempted, in respect of income required for absolute necessaries. Bentham recommended that a minimum of income, say £50 a year, should be left untaxed, on the principle now adopted in some cases under the Income Tax. If we had nothing but direct taxation, such a rule might be practicable. But with indirect taxation it is impossible. For how is the minimum to be secured against taxation? Even if this could be done, the determination of the proper amount of minimum would give rise to endless difficulties.

Modes of relieving the Poor.

Hence, under our existing taxation, another method is requisite. Exempt the necessaries themselves from taxation, and the poor man's ex-

The Principles of Taxation. 13

penditure on them will also be exempted. This secures in the most certain manner the application of the remission to the object intended, and it is the principle adopted in our own fiscal system. With it is properly joined the converse rule of taxing heavily those articles which are perverted into bad habits, and thus making the public revenue a means of their discouragement.

Modified in this sense, Adam Smith's rules of taxation may thus be expressed:—

1. Expenditure on bare necessaries should be exempt from taxation.

2. Expenditure on bad habits may be heavily taxed.

3. On the rest of his income every man ought to be taxed in an equal per centage.

4. Taxes ought to be certain and uniform, not arbitrary and unequal.

5. Every tax ought to be levied at the time and in the manner most convenient to the contributor.

6. Every tax ought to take out of the pockets of the people as little as possible beyond its produce to the Treasury.

Such a system might produce in the three examples above mentioned something like the following results, assuming that the taxpayers were

[margin: Chap. II. Adam Smith's rules modified. See "Wealth of Nations," Book V. chap. ii. part 2. Effects of such a system.]

men of moderate indulgence in the luxuries of their stations :—

	£	s.
A Wealthy Man with £5,000 a-year	500	0
A Professional Man or Tradesman with £500 a-year	45	0
A Workman with £50 a-year	3	10

The diminution in favour of the temperate part of the community would under this system be paid by an increased taxation on the bad habits of the intemperate.

These sums are the *average* of all Classes of Incomes of equal amounts; and will need variation for the different Classes of Incomes derived from Land, Personalty, and Industry.

CHAPTER III.

THE MODES OF TAXATION.

BY what methods can sums like these be raised from millions of Taxpayers? <small>Chap. III.</small>

Will any one Tax be adequate to the task? Suppose that Adam Smith's principle were adopted of an equal per centage on all classes, and that the amount was levied by an Income Tax of 10 per cent. on every kind of income. How long would its collection be possible? The unpopularity of such a mode of exaction would be formidable, even among the well-to-do classes. But among the poorer portion of the population it would be simply impracticable, the instalments would constantly be in arrear, and the arrears irrecoverable. The experience of mankind has always been that the load must be broken up and diffused among many Taxes. <small>Direct Taxation by one Tax impracticable.</small>

The burden of Taxation may be compared to the soldier's knapsack, a burden with which he cannot <small>A system of Taxes necessary.</small>

be allowed to dispense, and on which the ingenuity of centuries has been expended in devising means of lessening its hardship. A single strap is out of the question, as it would throw all the weight upon one place, and soon become intolerable. A system of straps is necessary to divide and equalize the pressure. Many systems have been invented by the wisdom of successive ages, but all have some drawback, and there is a long list of heart complaints, lung diseases, and cripplings which result from the pressure of the straps on one or other vital part or member.

Just so with Taxation, the heavy burden which must be borne by every nation, and which requires the greatest skill in its adjustment and fastening, to prevent its crippling the unhappy bearers. A single tax would be intolerable, and a system of taxes is necessary to distribute the weight more equably over the body corporate. Many systems have been devised, but they have generally been most unfortunate, hampering and disabling rather than assisting the sufferer, and many have been the national diseases and atrophies which have resulted from them. The fiscal straps have been multiplied to hundreds and even thousands, enveloping and shackling every limb and movement; round the arms, preventing their free use in industry; round

The Modes of Taxation.

the body, stopping its circulation and healthy action; and surrounding the head with an intricate and tantalising network through which light, air, and food could only penetrate in diminished quantities. The removal of these restrictions has been for years the labour of our statesmen, and there is still work to do in completing their reformation.

But skill may also be shown in lightening the knapsack, by providing less cumbrous and better necessaries, which may enable the soldier to do his work equally well with less expenditure of labour. The General or Statesman who can accomplish this, without sacrifice of efficiency, deserves the gratitude of his country.

The Taxes of the United Kingdom are still numerous, though very much fewer than those which existed in 1841. How can they be presented in the most clear and simple order? *British Taxes.*

The Imperial Taxes are distinguished in the public accounts under eight heads, *Customs, Excise, Stamps, Assessed Taxes, Income and Property Tax, Post Office, Crown Lands,* and *Miscellaneous.* But some of these heads include different kinds of Taxes, with no relationship except in the mode of their collection. They are, in fact, accidental divisions, handed down to us from remote history. *Their historical names.*

The Modes of Taxation.

CHAP. III.
Customs.

Custom duties existed in England before the Conquest, and derived their name from having been immemorially or customarily charged on exportation or importation of articles across the seas, or conveyance over bridges or ferries; and they were mentioned in Magna Charta. They now include only a few but most important imports.

Excise.

Excise duties were introduced in 1626, and were taxes excised (*excisa*) or cut off from articles of inland or home production. Though soon repealed, they were again introduced by a Parliamentary ordinance in 1643, imposing duties on ale, beer, cider, and perry, and thenceforth took a permanent place in our taxation. Besides articles of home production, they now include Licenses for their sale, Taxes on Public Carriages and Railways, Game Certificates, and the Tax on Dogs.

Assessed Taxes.

Assessed Taxes (*assessa* or *assessata*) date from *fumage* or smoke-farthings, paid as early as the Conquest to the King for every chimney. The custom fell into disuse, but was revived as a Hearth-tax by Charles II., and again enacted in the form of House and Window taxes by William III.

Stamps.

Stamp duties were invented in Holland during her great contest with Spain, and were the result of a large reward or prize offered to the person who should devise the best new tax. The *vectigal*

The Modes of Taxation. 19

chartæ, or Stamp duty, was suggested and approved in 1624 ; but was not introduced in England till 1671, or charged on Probates till 1694. The duties are heterogenous in their nature, comprising not only Stamps on deeds and bills, but Insurances, Probates, Legacy and Succession Duties, a number of Licences, and the tax on patent medicines.

The Income Tax was, I believe, invented in 1798, by Mr. Pitt.

The Local Taxes or Rates are probably the oldest of any, being the successors of the old County Rates, which were levied under the Heptarchy.

Thus the divisions of our taxation are in the highest degree historical, but of little use for purposes of analysis, since both the Excise and Stamps include so many taxes of different natures.

I turn next to Political Economy. Taxes are defined in the works of political economists with scientific accuracy—taxes on rent, taxes on land, taxes on profits, taxes on wages, taxes on income, taxes on commodities, taxes on contracts, taxes on communication, law taxes, and local taxes. But, though admirable for philosophical purposes, such a classification is too intricate and subtle for a practical treatise, where it is necessary to present

CHAP. III. some clear and broad outline which may readily impress itself upon the memory.

Direct and Indirect Taxation. One of the oldest and most simple definitions divides all Taxes into the two heads of *Direct* and *Indirect Taxation; Direct Taxes* being those which are paid by the person himself, who is meant to be the real contributor,—such as Assessed Taxes ; and *Indirect* being those which are paid by an intermediary, who reimburses himself from the real contributor,—such as the Customs and Excise Duties. But this definition cannot furnish us with a trustworthy classification, since it is founded upon an accident in the manner of payment, and not upon the nature of the Taxes themselves. The Income and Property Tax, for instance, is Direct Taxation when paid by the Owner himself, and Indirect when paid by the Tenant or Mortgagor.

Classification proposed. But there is another classification of Taxation, simple and easy of remembrance, and founded upon a radical difference in the nature of the Taxes themselves, but which has not hitherto been adopted in treatises on Political Economy :—

Taxation on Income and Expenditure. 1. *Taxes on Income and Property,* i.e. on *Receipts.*

2. *Taxes on Expenditure,* i.e. on *Outgoings.*

Both have existed from the remotest periods of

our history; the first in the County Rates, the second in the Customs; and both have been marvellously developed by the ingenuity of civilization. The first correspond most nearly with the feudal principle of Direct Taxation, the second with the earliest form of Indirect Taxation. The first are obligatory, and can scarcely be escaped by persons who possess the taxable amount of property or income; the second are to a large extent optional, since they may be largely reduced or avoided by those who are willing to forego expenditure.

Most of our *Imperial Taxes* may be ranged under one or other of these two heads; but there is one class of them that falls sometimes on Income and sometimes on Expenditure, and which I will put separately, as :— {Imperial Taxes.}

3. *Licenses and Taxes on Trades and Professions, and Intercourse.*

They were (curiously enough) imposed as Direct Taxes by our feudal predecessors, but have generally been considered Indirect Taxes by political economists, whether with sufficient reason remains to be discussed.

Our *Local Taxes* are also of a mixed character, falling sometimes on the Income of the Landlord, and sometimes on the Expenditure of the Tenant. {Local Taxes.}

CHAP. III. The determination of the proportion in which they are so divided is one of the most difficult and important questions in political Economics. I will place them under a separate head :—

4. *Local Rates and Tolls;*

and endeavour to separate them into their component parts in a subsequent chapter.

CHAPTER IV.

THE NOMINAL AND ACTUAL TAXATION OF THE UNITED KINGDOM.

I MUST now ask for indulgence while I go through the existing Taxes of the United Kingdom, and point out under which heads they should be arranged. The task may be tedious, but it is necessary to be performed if we would have a clear idea of the proportions which the different Taxes bear to one another, and of their correspondence or failure to correspond with the resources of the State.

But let us first determine how much of the Revenue is really Taxation. During the last nine years the Public Revenue has averaged £70,000,000 annually, and the Local Taxation has been increasing every year till it is now estimated at £22,500,000, making a total Nominal Taxation

Nominal Taxation.

of £92,500,000. The amounts for the financial year 1867-8, ending 5th April, 1868, were:

		£
Public Revenue	. . .	£69,600,000
Local Revenue	. . .	22,500,000
Total	. . .	£92,100,000

Revenue not derived from Taxation. But in this amount are included the rents or produce of the *Crown Lands*, which are national property; the *Post Office*, which is a business, carried on at extremely low charges, the actual cost of which cannot be considered as a tax; *Harbour Dues and Tolls*, for a similar reason; *Corporation Property;* and *Miscellaneous*, consisting chiefly of Indian repayments, old stores, and other waifs and strays. Their amounts for 1867-8 were :—

	£	£
Public Revenue—		
Crown Lands	340,000	
Post-office (Total cost of Service)	3,230,000	
Miscellaneous. . . .	2,590,000	
Local Revenue—		
Corporation Property	500,000	
Harbour Dues .	2,340,000	
		9,000,000
Revenue from Taxation. Leaving the Revenue derived from Taxation as		£83,100,000

Or a little more than 10⅓ per cent. on the £800,000,000 Gross Income of the nation.

But even this sum of £83,000,000 is not the real amount of Taxation, since part is derived from Taxes paid by Government officials, Fund-holders, soldiers, and others who are supported by Taxation. The net amount of actual Taxation is probably about £76,000,000, paid out of a gross Income (excluding everything received from the Government) of £720,000,000.

Actual Taxation.

But for practical purposes this distinction must be disregarded, since it is impossible to draw the line between Taxes paid out of taxes and those paid by the general income of the community.

We may, therefore, consider £83,000,000 as the present Taxation of the United Kingdom, and proceed to ascertain the sources from which it is drawn.

CHAPTER V.

TAXES ON INCOME AND PROPERTY.

<small>Chap. V.</small>

<small>See "National Income," pp. 64, 65.</small>

The first class of Taxes are those on Income and Property, which are borne for the most part by Incomes above £100, estimated to amount to £400,000,000 a-year, forming the upper half of the gross Income of the nation. They may be distinguished into two subdivisions, those paid out of Income, and those payable out of Capital.

1.—Taxes paid out of Income.

These include

<small>Taxes on Income.</small>

(1) *The Income and Property Tax*, which is not so much a Tax as a Code of Taxes, bringing within its jurisdiction Income of every description, from Land, from Houses, from Farming, from the Funds, from Trades and Professions, and from public Salaries and Pensions; and producing, in 1867-8, at the rate of 5*d*. in the pound, or 2 per cent. £6,177,000

(2) The *Land Tax* is an old Tax, originally 4*s*. in the pound, on the annual value of land, but which was made a fixed amount, and is constantly lessened by redemption. It now averages nearly 1 per cent. on the rental of the Land and Houses of the United Kingdom, and produces . 1,093,000

(3) *Law Funds and Fees*, which are taxes upon Income or Capital, and produce	218,000
The total of this sub-division is .	£7,488,000

2.—Taxes payable out of Capital.

We now come to the Taxes which are payable out of the *corpus* of property before the successor enters upon its enjoyment. It is evident that the successor loses two things: first, the portion of Capital abstracted by the Tax, and second, the annual income for the rest of his life which that portion would have produced. Such a Tax is heavier than an Income Tax of equal per centage, because the latter leaves the Capital untouched for the next successor. Suppose for instance, Probate or Administration Duty of 2 per cent. paid on £100,000 of Capital, amounting to £2,000; the successor loses during his life (if the fund produces $4\frac{1}{2}$ per cent.) £90 a year, which is more than 2 per cent. on the income of the remaining £98,000; and he has also lost £2,000 of Capital, which an Income Tax of 2 per cent. would have left in his possession. Reckoning the average enjoyment of property at thirty-three years, and the rate of interest on personalty at $4\frac{1}{2}$ per cent. I find from the tables that this is a loss represented by $1\frac{1}{2}$ per cent. per annum, or £30 a-year on £2,000, that being the annual payment which would in thirty-three years replace the Capital paid. Hence the effect of paying Probate Duty out of Capital is to increase the annual loss from the tax by one-third; so that Probate and Administration Duty, which averages 2 per cent. on the Capital assessed, is really a tax of £2 13s. 4d. per cent. upon the annual Income of the Taxpayer.

In a large number of cases the Probate, Legacy, and Succession Duties are paid by instalments out of income. But this involves a reduction of expenditure during the payment which causes a loss to the revenue.

I draw the conclusion that, if true economy is studied, Taxes payable out of Capital ought not to be applied to current expenditure, since, by destroying Capital, or diminishing other taxes, they cost the country more than a tax upon income of equal produce. They ought to be devoted to the reduction of the National Debt, so as permanently to lessen the annual burden of the nation in proportion to the diminution of the Capital of her citizens. These Taxes are :—

(4) *Probate Duty* on Wills and Administrations of all personal property. It averages 2 per cent. on the Capital assessed, or 2¾ on its life income, and produced in 1867-8, with *Fee Stamps* £1,773,000

(5) *Legacy Duty*, which is paid in addition to Probate Duty on all legacies and residuary bequests of Personalty,

and on all Real Property devised for sale, except by wives or husbands, and which averages 2½ per cent. on the Capital assessed, or 3⅓ per cent. on its life income, and produced in 1867-8 2,162,000

(6) *Succession Duty*, which is levied on all successions to real Property and settled Personalty, exempting wives and husbands. It charges the interest of every successor to property as a life estate, and is less onerous than Legacy Duty, averaging only 1¼ per cent. on the capitalized value of the Life Income, and therefore on the Income itself. It produced in the same year . . . 721,000

(7) *Stamps on Deeds and other Instruments.* These are principally Taxes on transfers of property, and in a large proportion of cases are paid out of Capital. But being paid in small sums and at irregular intervals no rule can be laid down respecting their extra cost to the tax-payer. They are rather more than one-third per cent. on £400,000,000 Income amounting to 1,602,000

The Total of the Taxes paid out of Capital is therefore £6,258,000

The total amount of all the Taxes on Income and Property is £13,746,000, or rather less than 3½ per cent. on £400,000,000, of which nearly 2 per cent. is paid out of Income, and 1½ per cent. is payable out of Capital.

CHAPTER VI.

TAXES ON EXPENDITURE.

Chap. VI. THE second class of Taxes consists of two main divisions, *Taxes on Establishments*, as houses, servants, carriages, &c.; and *Taxes on Food and Stimulants;* the latter including tea and coffee, alcoholic drinks, and tobacco. They include the larger portion of the three important heads of Assessed Taxes, Customs, and Excise.

1. TAXES ON ESTABLISHMENTS.

On Establishments. These fall almost exclusively upon houses above £20 rent, and their occupiers, with incomes above £100 a-year, forming the upper £400,000,000 of the Income of the nation.

(1) *The Assessed Taxes*, which charge Houses above £20 Rent, Menservants, Carriages, Horses, and Armorial Bearings. The House Tax is uniform at 9*d.* in the pound on all Houses, and half that amount on all shops at and

Taxes on Expenditure. 31

and above £20, and probably does not fall upon the landlord. The tax on horses includes those kept for trade purposes. These Taxes amounted in 1867-8, to . . £2,360,000

Very similar to them are the *Taxes on Race-horses and Plate*, and the *Game* and *Dog Licences*, the latter including agricultural dogs. They produced . . . 590,000

(2) *The Fire Insurance Duties*, a Tax on the buildings and moveable property of prudent people. It is a duty of 1s. 6d. per cent. on the capital value of the property insured. A prudent man will have an Insurance of £2,000 for house and furniture, where his house-rent is £100 a year. The duty on this would be 30s. a year. Hence I calculate that Insurance is a tax of 1½ per cent. on an insurer's rent. The Tax produced in 1867-8 £974,000, which, less £300,000 Trade Insurance, is . 674,000

TOTAL . £3,624,000

Being nearly one per cent. on £400,000,000.

2. TAXES ON FOOD AND STIMULANTS.

They will be most clearly understood if arranged in three subdivisions.

On Food and Stimulants.

(3) *Taxes on Necessaries*, or substantial food :—

Of these only one is left in the Statute Book, the duty on *Corn*, of a shilling per quarter, which produced in 1867—8 . . . . £870,000

(4) *Taxes on Semi-Necessaries*, or wholesome adjuncts of food, the use of which has within the last century become almost a second nature with both sexes and every class of our fellow-countrymen.

Dr. E. Smith, "Practical Dietary," p. 99.

Chap. VI. But they are acquired habits, and are said by medical writers on diet to be inferior in nutriment to the milk of former days. These Taxes are on :—

Tea, which at 6*d.* per lb. produced in 1867-8	£2,827,000
Coffee, Chicory, and *Cocoa,* which produced	550,000
Sugar, which is a valuable addition to food, especially for children, contains little nutriment in proportion to price as compared with wheat-flour or milk, and is considered as a luxury by almost all classes. The Duty in 1867-8 averaged 1*d.* per lb., and produced	5,646,000
With these articles may be conveniently joined imported *Fruits, Sago,* &c., which are articles of food, though more distinctly luxuries than Sugar. They produced	447,000
The Total of this subdivision is	£9,470,000

(5) *Taxes on Alcoholic Liquors and Tobacco.*— These are unquestionably luxuries, and, when used in excess, become unwholesome to the consumer, and productive of evil to the nation. The taxes on them are heavy, in order to prevent this excess. They are :—

Wine, which, at an average duty of 2*s.* per gallon, produced in 1867-8	£1,470,000
Beer, which is taxed in the *Malt* 2*s.* 8½*d.* per bushel, and, at the average production of 18 gallons of beer per bushel, pays 1½*d.* per gallon, and produced	6,300,000
Spirits, of which the British pay to the Excise £10,510,000, and the Foreign pay to the Customs £4,300,000 by duties which average 10*s.* per gallon, making a total of	14,810,000
Tobacco, which at an average duty of 3*s.* 4*d.* per lb., produces	6,540,000
The Total of this subdivision is	£29,120,000

The totals of these Taxes on Food and Stimulants are £39,560,000.

They form nearly half the actual Taxation, both Imperial and Local, of the United Kingdom, and are nearly 5 per cent. on the £800,000,000 gross Income of the nation. Of this total, the Necessaries and Semi-Necessaries amount to £10,340,000, or 1¼ per cent., while Alcoholic Liquors and Tobacco amount to £29,126,000, or nearly 3¾ per cent.

The latter is therefore an Income Tax paid in hard cash to the Treasury through the medium of the retailer, amounting to 10*d.* in the pound on the gross Income of every man, woman, and child in the United Kingdom.

CHAPTER VII.

TAXES ON TRADES, PROFESSIONS, AND INTERCOURSE.

<small>Chap. VII.</small> The third class of Taxes includes those which have been imposed on particular trades and professions, mostly in the form of Licences, but sometimes in the form of Taxes, such as that on Railway receipts. It appears to have been a maxim of Government in the olden days that dealers in taxable commodities must themselves be taxed for the privilege of selling articles of such increased value, while dealers in untaxed commodities might escape scot free. Thus tea-dealers and wine-merchants had to take out licences, while ironmongers and drapers needed none. The first were doubly taxed, on their goods and power of sale, so narrowing both their circle of customers and their profits; the latter were exempt from taxes on either head.

<small>Origin of Licences.</small>

<small>Sub-divisions.</small> These Taxes may be arranged in five sub-divisions :—

Professions, and Intercourse.

(1) *Professions and ordinary Trades—*
Attorneys and Conveyancers, Bankers, Auctioneers, Gold and Silver Plate-dealers, Pawnbrokers, Hawkers, Cardmakers, Patent Medicines, Vinegar, Soap, and Paper Makers, Patents for Inventions, and Tea and Coffee Dealers, paying in 1867-8 . . . . £576,000

(2) *Mercantile—*
Bills of Exchange £820,000
Receipts and Drafts 562,000
Marine Insurances and some Customs charges and part Fire Insurance . 567,000
——— 1,949,000

(3) *Dealers in Alcohol and Tobacco—*
Wine-sellers £132,000
Brewers, Maltsters, and Beer-sellers . 750,000
Spirit-sellers and Distillers . . . 705,000
Tobacco-dealers and Manufacturers . 81,000
——— 1,668,000

(4) *Conveyance and Miscellaneous—*
Posthorses and Public Carriages . . £284,000
Railways 486,000
Post-office (surplus over cost) . . 1,517,000
Miscellaneous 80,000
——— 2,367,000

£6,560,000

Thus forming a total of £6,560,000, or more than three-fourths per cent. on the gross income of the nation. *Total of these Taxes.*

By whom are these duties really paid? The question has received many answers, some economists maintaining that they are all paid by the customer or consumer, others that they are borne by the dealer. But each trade must be judged by its own circumstances. *Are they paid by the trader or the public?*

Chap. VII.

Paid by the trader, and therefore by Income.

The professions and many ordinary trades, and the tea and coffee dealers, generally pay the tax out of Income, without being able to raise their prices to the public, either from the existence of a legal maximum, or from the prices being fixed by the competition of the large dealers, on whom the licence is no appreciable burden.

Receipts and draft stamps are chiefly a tax upon the Income of retail traders, being too small in each instance to be recovered from the public.

Railways and public carriages are obliged, to a great extent, themselves to bear the contributions levied from them, from the existence of maximum charges limited by law or by the public capacity of paying.

Paid by the public, and therefore by Expenditure.

On the other hand, bills of exchange are part of the expenses of commerce, and are added by merchants to the wholesale or retail prices.

So also the monopoly enjoyed by brewers, beer-sellers, spirit sellers, tobacco dealers, wine sellers, and pawnbrokers, must enable them to charge the cost of their licence upon their customers; thus adding from 5 to 10 per cent. to the heavy Customs and Excise duties. In a subsequent chapter I shall show the increase of prices to the public to be very far in excess of these amounts.

The Post-office surplus is also a tax upon expenditure.

CHAPTER VIII.

LOCAL RATES AND TOLLS.

THIS department of our Taxation is rendered uncertain by local mists and gloom, which hang over many of the cities and towns of England, and brood in thick and impenetrable obscurity over the whole of Scotland, so that we cannot obtain a clear idea of the extent of the burden and of its features. The old Saxon dislike of centralization shows itself as strongly as ever, preventing the transmission of information and fostering all sorts of inequalities and anomalies. Probably there are not two parishes in England where the local rates are identical, and the differences are frequently enormous. The property on which they are levied is nearly as follows:— *[marginal note: Chap. VIII. Obscurity of Local Taxation.]*

	Rental.	Rateable Value.	
England (Poor Rate) . . .	£110,000,000	£94,000,000	Electoral Returns, 1866.
Scotland (estimate) . . .	16,000,000	14,000,000	
Ireland (estimate as to Rent) .	15,500,000	13,000,000	
	£141,500,000	£121,000,000	

CHAP. VIII.
Local Taxation Returns, 1868.
Do. Ireland.

So far as the total taxation and expenditure can be ascertained, they may be divided into the following heads. The amounts are for the year ending June 1867 for England, and 1865 for Ireland. For Scotland, which vouchsafes no information except as to Poor Rates, they are estimated on the same proportionate scale as in the other two countries.

(1) *Relief of the Poor*—

		£	
Expenditure in England	.	6,960,000	
Scotland	.	808,000	
Ireland	.	797,000	
			8,565,000

This is an average charge of 6 per cent. on the Rental, or 7 per cent. (1s. 5d. in the pound) on Rateable value.

(2) *County Expenditure*—
County and Police Rates, Highway Rates and Tolls, Sewers, Drainage, and Embankments, Bridges, and part of Church Rates—

		£	
England	. . . .	4,298,000	
Scotland (estimate)	. . .	550,000	
Ireland (including three-fourths of Grand Jury Cess)	. . .	872,000	
			5,720,000

(3) *Town Expenditure*—
Local Management, Corporations, Borough Rates, Improvement Commissioners, Local Boards, Lighting, Markets and Fairs, and part of Church Rates—

England	. . .	4,510,000	
(including £500,000 Corporation property.)			
Carried forward	. . . .		£14,285,000

Local Rates and Tolls.

	£	£
Brought forward	4,510,000	14,285,000
Scotland (estimate)	650,000	
Ireland (including one-fourth of Grand Jury Cess)	780,000	
		5,940,000

Besides this there are:

(4) *Navigation Dues*—
Harbour Dues, Pilotage, and Light Dues—

	£	£
England	1,872,000	
Scotland (estimate)	250,000	
Ireland	213,000	
		2,335,000
Total Local Revenue		**£22,560,000**

The above is raised nearly as follows:—

	£	£
Taxation—		
Rates	18,500,000	
Tolls, &c.	1,225,000	
		19,725,000
Other Revenue—		
Corporation Property	500,000	
Navigation Dues	2,335,000	
		2,835,000
		£22,560,000

Hence the Local Rates amount to £18,500,000, and form an average charge of 13 per cent. on the £140,000,000 Rental of the United Kingdom, or 15 per cent. (3s. in the pound) on the Rateable value of £120,000,000. But in practice they vary from 6d. in the pound up to 10s. or even more.

CHAPTER IX.

SUMMARY OF TAXATION.

Chap. IX. Such is a brief classification of the Taxes of the United Kingdom. The following Table will show them in a more compact form:

IMPERIAL TAXATION, 1867—8.

I. Taxes on Income and Property *solely*.

Payable out of Income—

Income and Property Tax	£6,177,000
Land Tax	1,093,000
Law Funds and Fees	218,000
	£7,488,000

Payable out of Capital—

Probate Duty	£1,773,000
Legacy Duty	2,162,000
Succession Duty	721,000
Stamps on Deeds	1,602,000
	£6,258,000

Total on Income and Property solely . **£13,746,000**

Summary of Taxation.

II. TAXES ON EXPENDITURE *solely.*

Establishments—

Assessed Taxes	£2,360,000	
Racehorses, Plate, Game Licenses, Dogs	590,000	
Fire Insurance (less Trade portion) .	674,000	
	£3,624,000	

Corn, Tea, &c.—

Necessaries (Corn)	£870,000	
Semi-Necessaries (Tea, Coffee, and Sugar)	9,470,000	
	10,340,000	
Tobacco and Alcohol . .	29,120,000	
Total on Expenditure solely . . .	£43,084,000	

III. TAXES ON TRADES AND PROFESSIONS AND INTERCOURSE.

Professions and Ordinary Trades .	£576,000	
Mercantile	1,949,000	
Alcohol and Tobacco Licenses . .	1,668,000	
Conveyances, &c.	2,367,000	
		6,560,000
TOTAL IMPERIAL TAXATION .		£63,390,000

LOCAL TAXATION, 1865—7.

IV. LOCAL TAXATION AND TOLLS.

Relief of Poor	£8,565,000	
County Rates and Tolls . . .	5,720,000	
Town Rates (less Corporation Property)	5,440,000	
		19,725,000
TOTAL ACTUAL TAXATION .	. .	£83,115,000

CHAP. IX.   Brought forward   .   .   .   £83,115,000
           V. REVENUE NOT FROM TAXATION.

               IMPERIAL—
                   Post Office (actual cost) .   .   . £3,230,000
                   Crown Lands   340,000
                   Miscellaneous   2,590,000
                                                    ─────────
                                                    6,160,000
               LOCAL—
                   Corporation Property   . £500,000
                   Harbour Dues   .   .   . 2,340,000
                                              ─────────
                                              2,840,000
                                                           ─────────
                                                           9,000,000
                                                           ─────────
                        TOTAL REVENUE   . £92,115,000

PART II.

Distribution and Pressure of Taxation.

CHAPTER X.

THE PRESSURE OF TAXATION.

SUPPOSE the Prince of some feudal island, the sole proprietor of its soil, surrounded by a numerous tenantry, of every degree of rank and fortune— great vassals enjoying wide domains, farmers of more moderate means, traders dwelling in the towns, and labourers of all grades of skill and earnings—from whom he drew annual rents for their lands and houses, out of which were defrayed the whole expense of government, of the military forces, of ships of war, of the civil administration, and the maintenance of the destitute. Would it not be his duty, as a wise and just ruler, to ascertain by every means in his power that all his tenants were paying fair and equitable rents proportioned to the value of their holdings? *The advisability of inquiry.*

It might probably have happened that in ruder times his ancestors had fixed the assessments of his subjects in a rough and unequal manner, either through ignorance of the capabilities of the soil, or inaptitude for calculation, or from personal favouritism. But he would rightly say that the existence of such inequalities was no reason for their continuance, and that increasing knowledge and juster ideas of the obligations of a ruler render it his duty to order a thorough revaluation of the country, and to remove all causes of complaint.

It might possibly be represented for his more powerful vassals that they should be exempted from paying a full rental, because they were large employers of labourers, through the rent of whose cottages they made vicarious payment; and that it was for the good of the country to encourage such employment. But the reply would be that rent paid direct by servants out of their own earnings could not be accepted in exoneration of that which ought to be paid direct by their masters.

It might, on the other hand, be urged on the behalf of the labourers that they as poor men ought to have houses rent-free, and leave the burden of the State to the rich. But it would be answered that no man who was able to labour ought to owe his home or personal protection to the charity of others, or to

The Pressure of Taxation.

throw upon them his fair share of the burden; but that every individual, in just proportion to his ability, ought to contribute to the expenses of the State.

Similar reasons should influence a nation in regard to Taxation. It is said that there is no use in inquiring into the incidence of Taxation; that Taxes have always been imposed in a rough and ready manner, without looking narrowly into the comparative burdens which they impose; and that such a scrutiny is too minute for the dignity of statesmanship. But no inquiry into details is beneath the dignity of Statesmen if it affects the well-being of a people, or is likely to introduce greater justice and fairness into the financial government of the country.

So, again, it is sometimes argued that the taxation of persons employed, even when paid independently, ought to be counted as the taxation of their employers, in order that the latter may be encouraged in giving liberal employment. But rich men are not the only employers of labour. Every workman, in respect of the articles that he consumes, is an employer of the producer, and would on such a supposition be equally entitled to claim the benefit of the producer's taxation. A thousand workmen, each with £70 a year of

Primary Taxation alone to be counted.

CHAP. X. earnings, are as large and far more constant an employer than a single millionaire with £70,000 a year income. Every man, in equal proportion, according to his ability, is bound to pay his own primary taxation, that is to say, the taxation due upon his own property and household; and has no right to count towards this debt any secondary taxation, that is to say, taxation of other people to which he contributes by paying their earnings. The test must always be, Who would receive the benefit if the taxes were remitted? The person benefited is the real taxpayer. Thus a gamekeeper is employed by a country gentleman at weekly wages, but lives in his own cottage, and pays his own taxes on beer and sugar. If the taxes are taken off, he reaps the benefit, and is therefore the true payer. But a house-servant, if his provisions are found for him, would receive no benefit, so that his master is the taxpayer.

All Classes interested in the inquiry. It is sometimes suggested in a tone of warning that it is not wise to stir the question of the incidence of taxation, for that the propertied classes are interested in keeping things as they are. But the propertied classes are above all things interested in removing any well-grounded dissatisfaction, and thus increasing the stability of our institutions. Let the subject be fully and fairly investigated in the interest of the nation, endeavouring to arrive truthfully at the actual facts, and the result will promote the welfare and security of all classes of society.

CHAPTER XI.

TAXES ON PROPERTY DO NOT BECOME RENT CHARGES.

<small>CHAP. XI.</small>　A STRANGE theory forms the groundwork of many
<small>The Rent Charge Theory.</small>　writings on Taxation—that taxes on property, when old-established obligations, cease to be taxes on the owner, and become independent rent charges
<small>Land Tax.</small>　belonging to the State. Thus, the Land Tax, though originally imposed distinctly as taxation, is said to be now no burden upon the Landowner, but a share in the property which belongs to the
<small>Poor Rate.</small>　State. So the Poor Rate, though re-imposed in varying proportions at annual or half-yearly sessions, is maintained to be, so far as it falls upon the landlord, a charge upon the land, which forms no part of his estate, and in which he has
<small>Succession, Probate, and Legacy Duties.</small>　no interest. So also the Succession Duty on land, and the Probate and Legacy Duties on personalty, are contended to be portions appropriated by the

State in return for leave to inherit, and to be the condition of a boon rather than the burden of a tax.

It is urged in support of this theory that, on the purchase or sale of landed property, the Land Tax and Poor Rates are allowed for and deducted as mortgages, so that the purchaser receives a net income for his purchase-money, clear of these charges. It follows as a logical consequence of the theory that the owner of land or personal property, being really not taxed by any of these taxes, ought to be taxed again on his net income, in the same per centage as, or larger than, the possessor of an untaxed industrial income. *Owner would have to be taxed again.*

But, to make a matter clear, there is nothing like an example; and we can find a very good one, of first-rate magnitude, in our Local Taxation. The principle will apply to any of the others. We have seen that the gross rental assessed to these taxes is £140,000,000, and that the Local Rates amount to £18,500,000. Let us assume, for the sake of argument, what may afterwards be shown to be probable, that £12,000,000 of this amount comes out of the pockets of the Landlords. Then, if the theory is correct, the owners of this property, worth a rental of 140 millions, are not taxed in one farthing of the twelve millions by which their *Example in Local Rates.*

CHAP. XI. rents are diminished, but this large amount is a rent charge belonging to the State, and with which they have nothing to do. It follows necessarily that, in justice to the other taxpayers, the Owners ought to be taxed again to make up their full quota of 10 per cent. of Taxation. Suppose, again, for the sake of argument, that the deficiency below this quota is 7 per cent. on £140,000,000 or £10,000,000. Then this additional ten millions ought at once to be imposed on the Landlords and their successors, and levied, as all taxes on property must, to be effectual, "at the source," *i.e.* on the property itself. The gross amount payable to the State will thus become £22,000,000, in respect of £140,000,000 of rental.

The same state again recurs. But changes of property are continually occurring both by deaths and sales. Every heir would inherit subject to the increased taxation, which would therefore, on the reasoning of the theory, constitute a rent charge due to the State. Every purchaser would deduct the whole outgoings from the price, and take care to secure a net income at 3 per cent. on his purchase money. Hence after a certain lapse of time, when these changes have become universal, the old state of things recurs. The Owners have bought or inherited subject to the £22,000,000 rent charge, and by the theory must be held to be unaffected by it. Not a penny of the £22,000,000, if the theory is correct, can be held to be their Taxation. So that we must tax them again, in another 7 per cent. on the net rental, so making up a gross assessment of £31,000,000 on the gross rental of £140,000,0000.

But no sooner has this been done than the same causes begin to operate, and the same circle to recur again and again; until it is demonstrable by the strictest rules of logic,—assuming the theory to be correct, and giving time for sufficient changes of property,—that in the course of successive generations the owners may pay £130,000,000 out of the £140,000,000 in Local Taxes, and yet by the theory be perfectly untaxed, and require taxing again on their £10,000,000 of net income!

The theory contains three errors or fallacies which lead to this absurd conclusion. The first is a fallacy as to the principle of inheritance. By the English laws, a man is allowed to hand down his money or land to his children with as complete proprietorship as he himself enjoyed it, so that the ownership of the children is the same as that of the father, and they cannot lose the *reversion* to the portion necessary to pay the tax. It remains always a tax, continuing during the will of the nation, and not a rentcharge which would be the perpetual property of the State.

<small>As to Purchasers' Investments.</small> The second fallacy is the assumption that purchasers always buy with deduction of the taxes, and so obtain a clear income on their purchase money. This is the object at which they aim, but every purchaser knows how often he fails in obtaining it. Rates have also a tendency to increase, and to form a fresh burden upon the property. And fresh capital is invested at every change of ownership, and during most ownerships, in improving the land and buildings.

<small>As to Purchase Money.</small> The third fallacy consists in the forgetfulness of the theorist that the purchase money must come from somewhere, and must itself have been subject to previous taxation. It may have come from sale of another landed estate, or houses, in which case it must have been realized at a loss which balances the deductions on the purchase. It may have come from personal property, in which case it was subject to Income Tax and Probate and Legacy Duty, and was diminished accordingly. Or it may have been savings from Income, in which case, according to our theorists, it has been more heavily taxed in its acquirement than either of the preceding properties. So that in every case the purchaser is merely exchanging one kind of taxation

for another when he buys property, and the new taxes are as really taxation as the old.

Hence Taxes on Property, of however long standing, must be counted as *bona fide* taxation of the Owners, just as much as if they were Taxes on Income or Expenditure.

But another theory now steps in. It is said on the high authority of Mr. Mill, "that land is an exception to the ordinary rule of Equality of Taxation, because, with the increase of population, it spontaneously increases in value, without exertion or sacrifice on the part of the owners, but with complete passiveness on their part; so that it would be no violation of the principles on which private property is grounded, if the State should appropriate this increase of wealth, or part of it, as it arises; instead of allowing it to become an unearned appendage to the riches of a particular class." Let us examine the soundness of the rule thus enunciated.

In other things than land could the State with justice lay down a principle of part appropriation of the spontaneous increase? Let us take one or two instances. A merchant sends out orders to his correspondent in China to buy a cargo of tea, and to insure and send it home to London. When the voyage from China to England is completed, and without much risk on the part of the owner, the tea

Chap. XI.

Mr. Mill, on the increased value of land. "Political Economy," Book V. c. ii. s. 5.

has increased in value, so as to afford a very handsome profit. Would any one propose to appropriate to the State any portion of this spontaneous increase? Again, a corn-merchant, with knowledge of a scanty harvest, buys and stores a large quantity of corn, and sells it in the spring at a considerable advance. Could the State justly demand to share any portion of this spontaneous increase? Again, a capitalist sees some open fields close to a thriving town, and buys them at the market price; and, after a greater or less term of waiting, is rewarded by resales as building ground at many times the former value. Could the State put in a claim for any portion of this profit? Or, once more, a landowner by a road or railway opens up his property, and at once doubles its letting value. Would this be a fair case for State participation?

Yet how does the case of the ordinary landowner differ? In neither case is there an absence of risk. Property often depreciates from local circumstances. In Ireland it has sometimes depreciated to a ruinous extent from national misfortunes or disturbances. In neither case is there an absence of foresight. The intending landowner buys with the knowledge that there is a strong probability of a rise in value, just like the China merchant or the corn-dealer, and he pays a higher price on that account, and is content with a smaller per centage on his money.' In both cases the increase depends upon the artificial protection of the State, and could not be obtained without it. The China merchant buys at Canton in security produced by the British fleet, and brings home his property in safety under the same protection. He warehouses it in London docks, he sells it to brokers, and he realizes his profit at his bankers through a most complex and artificial mechanism, which would tumble to pieces and deprive him of the last penny under a very easy amount of lawlessness.

All property is the creation and creature of the Law, and ought to be treated with equal justice. If part appropriation of its increase by the State is not fair towards one kind, neither can it be fair towards another. If part appropriation by means of greatly augumented taxes is not fair towards one kind, neither is it fair towards another. A policy of appropriation would be destructive of one of the main objects of property, since it would discourage improvements. Besides, if the increase is to be appropriated, a decrease must be guaranteed against by the State. As Mr. Mill says, "the present market price must be secured to them." Stripped to its kernel, Mr. Mill's theory is simply this, that landowners are only entitled in strictness to a

CHAP. XI. rent-charge upon their estates, and that the improving interest and its disposal is the property and prerogative of the State. But this is a clause out of a totally different creed as to the rights of property, and a different policy, from those which have formed the foundation of the laws of England.[1]

Surely the more sensible view must be that taxation should be regulated, to a certain extent, by the precariousness of property, so that an Industrial income, exposed to a hundred accidents, should be let off more lightly than Personal property; and Personal property, as more susceptible of diminution, should be taxed less heavily than the more stable and growing Landed estates. But all such differences should be moderate, so as not to become virtually exemptions, and they should not be greater for the higher classes of society than for the lower and more necessitous.

---

[1] How would London house proprietors and leaseholders like Mr. Mill's theory to be carried out, by a law that they should be entitled only to the present annual value of their houses, and that all future increase of value should belong to the State?

CHAPTER XII.

THE RATING QUESTION.

It is the custom in England to rate the Occupiers of land and houses, because, said Sir Cornewall Lewis, of the superior facility of collection. There is a person to come upon, and goods to seize, whereas the owner may be absent, and require tedious legal proceedings. Where these conditions failed, as in the case of the poorest classes, a custom grew up of throwing back the burden upon the Owners by the Compounding System. Under this system the Owner himself paid the rates, receiving a deduction for collecting them in his rents and for empty tenements. But whether the Overseer collects the money from the Occupier or whether from the Owner, out of whose pocket does the rate really come? Does the Occupier pay it as a clear addition to what would otherwise be his rent? Or is the Owner the real and ultimate payer out of what he could otherwise obtain as rent?

The Rating Question.

CHAP. XII.

As the Local Rates upon Occupiers and Owners amount to £18,500,000, the question is one of the utmost importance to our inquiry, in order that we may apportion this immense sum rightly among the taxpayers.

The subject divides itself into two branches—
(1) Rates upon Land or Farms,
(2) Rates upon Houses;
of which the first is the most simple, and throws light upon the second.

Rates upon Farms.

(1) As regards the Rates upon Land, which are paid by Farmers, there is a great concurrence of opinion that they fall chiefly upon Landlords, and diminish the Rent that would otherwise be paid. Land is a machine, capable of manufacturing a limited amount of produce, and the Rent that a Farmer can afford to pay is limited by that produce; so that everything that increases the expense of production reduces the surplus which is available for his own profit and the Landlord's rent. As the Farmer cannot live without a certain amount of profit, he endeavours in bargaining for a farm to deduct the whole of the rates from what in their absence he would have been willing to pay as rent. Does he always succeed?

Many eminent authorities maintain that he does. In valuing a farm for letting, as between landlord and tenant, a land-valuer always deducts the Local Rates to arrive at the fair Annual Rent. Land-valuers invariably answer that the landlord pays the rates. Farmers reply more cautiously that they always endeavour to deduct them. Sir Cornewall Lewis gave his opinion thus upon the point. Speaking of farmers, he said :—

Chap. XII. Mr. Clutton, Lords' Committee. Burdens on Land, 1846. Q. 5626.

"I have no doubt that the local rates, so far as they can be foreseen and calculated upon, are deductions from the landlord's rent. Though they are paid by the occupier, they enter into his calculation in arranging his rent with his landlord ; and, so far as the rates can be made a matter of precontract, I have no doubt they constitute a deduction from the rent. On the other hand, any sudden or unexpected increase of parochial expenditure would, until the contract was readjusted, fall entirely upon the tenant."

Lords' Committee on Parochial Assessments, 1850. Q. 32.

A very high authority on all matters of farming writes thus to me :—

"No doubt all the *increase* of rates falls upon the tenant, and that is no small amount. There is such a competition for land and houses, that, even where property is relet, the *old* rather than the *new rates* are supposed to belong to the landlord, and all the *fresh outgoings* to the tenant. You may fairly say that all the increase of rates within the last twenty-five years has fallen upon the occupier."

The following letter puts the question very practically, and is from a gentleman farming 400 acres in Kent :—

"There was last night a meeting of the Committee of our Chamber of Agriculture, and I wished to obtain other opinions than my own on the subject of Rates.

"The question produced, as I expected, some difference of opinion among those whom I considered the greatest authorities, land-agents holding that the rates are really paid by the landlord, and farmers maintaining that it is not so, but that they are paid by the tenant in a greater or less degree according to the circumstances of each case.

"When a farm is let by offer, the Offerers will of course ascertain the amount of burdens affecting it, and regulate the amount of their offers accordingly, though even in that case they are often induced to go beyond the mark from the fear that some one may outbid them.

"When again it is let privately, I believe that the landlord very often virtually says, 'I want as much rent for my land as I can get. I shall take so much and no less, and you may find out about the rates for yourself;" and I believe that the tenant, in his anxiety to get the farm, often takes the rates to a considerable extent upon himself.

"Besides this, the rates are not a fixed quantity. There is a constant tendency to increase, and in many cases a very rapid increase, while the rent remains the same, or is increased from time to time also."

Incidence of Rates on Land, three-fourths on Landlord, one-fourth on Tenant.

On all the evidence that I can collect, I have little doubt that, although in theory the rates are paid by the landlord, yet in practice, and on the average of tenancies, a portion of the rates does fall upon the tenant. Many practical men concur with me in thinking that the average incidence of rates is *three-fourths on the landlord,* and *one-fourth on the tenant,* and this calculation is adopted in the following pages.

Rates on Houses.

2. As regards Houses, the case is rather different, because the tenant is not limited by the produce.

The Rating Question.

He will pay for convenience, or from dislike of change, even an excessive rent. But, as in the case of farms, the valuers and house-agents are very unanimous in their opinion that the Rates are really paid by the Landlords. In proof, they quote cases of houses of exactly similar character, standing side by side or on opposite sides of the street, but in different parishes, where the rents are £20 or £30 higher or lower in exact proportion to the difference of rates.

The great authority of Sir G. C. Lewis is on the same side. In the same evidence, speaking of houses, he says :— *Q. 119.*

"I have no doubt that ultimately, in the great majority of cases, the incidence of the rate is upon the owner."

He also mentions the fact that where rates are excused on account of the poverty of the tenant, the landlord for the most part gets the full benefit of the remission, and raises his rent to the full amount remitted. This is the case at the present time in East London, and the utmost vigilance is required on the part of the parochial officers to prevent the excusal of tenants, who are sent by the landlords to make application to the magistrates, in order that the landlords may receive an increased rent for their property. The notoriousness of the practice is recited in the preamble of a clause in *Q. 136.*

CHAP. XII.
59 Geo. III. c. 12, s. 19.

the first Compounding Act, in 1819, as one of the chief reasons for its passing.

But, notwithstanding this array of authorities, I am disposed to think that a considerable part of the Rates is paid by the Occupiers, in addition to the Rent they would pay if Rates were abolished; and for the following reasons :—

A general and uniform tax does not, as a rule, affect the net price of the article on which it is placed. An irregular or partial tax does affect it. Thus, an excise tax on British spirits, without a countervailing customs' duty on the foreign, will lower the *net* price of British spirits. A uniform duty on both will either lower both equally, or lower neither. An increased duty on beer, without a similar increase on porter, would be likely to lower the net price of beer. An increased duty on both beer and porter would be likely to lower the net price of both (though not to the full extent of the tax), since the brewers might be able to put a part, but not the whole, of the increase on the public. A parallel case occurred during the rise of malt in the Crimean War.

The case of houses is very similar. Where rates are unequal in the same neighbourhood, or in accessible neighbourhoods, the net rent of the heavier-taxed house falls in proportion, and the surplus tax is paid by the landlord. But it does not follow that the portion which is common to both rates falls entirely upon the landlords. The house-tax of 9d. in the £1 on dwelling-houses above £20 is a uniform tax, and I believe that it is almost entirely a tenants' tax, and does not fall on the landlords. So also there is a certain amount of local rates, about 2s. in the £1, which is uniform all over the kingdom. I do not think that this portion falls wholly upon the landlords. There may be another 1s. or 1s. 6d. which is common to all parishes in large towns, and comes under the same principle.

In the better class of houses the *increase* of rates falls very much upon the tenants, in the manner described respecting farms by the two letters above quoted; and this increase is often large and rapid. London Occupiers tell me that their landlords require them to bear the increase, and raise their rents as well.

Parochial officers of large experience have told me that, if the rates were largely lessened, or thrown on the Consolidated Fund, the landlord would not obtain the whole benefit, though he might absorb the major part.

From these facts I come to the conclusion, in which I have the concurrence of men of great

66 *The Rating Question.*

<small>CHAP. XII.
Incidence of Rates on Houses, two-thirds on Landlord, one-third on Tenant.</small>

practical acquaintance with the subject, that on the average of House Property the incidence of Rates may be estimated at *two-thirds on the Landlord and one-third on the Tenant*, where the Rates are paid by the Tenant; but that the Landlord pays a larger proportion where they are compounded for by him.

<small>But calculated half to Landlord, half to Tenant.</small>

But, in order to avoid any under-estimate of the pressure of Taxation on the Tenant, I have, in the following pages, taken the Rates on Houses as paid *half by the Landlord and half by the Tenant;* and they will be so divided between those parties in the calculations of their Taxation.

<small>Town and Country Rates.
Sir M. H. Beach's Return, 53, 1868.</small>

The next point is to ascertain the proportion in which the Rates are divided between Town and Country. A return furnished last year divides the Rateable Value and Rates in England and Wales for 1865 as follows:—

RATEABLE VALUE.

(1) Metropolis	£14,021,000	
(2) Cities and Boroughs	17,290,000	
		31,311,000
(3) Counties		58,826,000
Total		£90,137,000

RATES.

(1) Metropolis	£2,839,000	
(2) Cities and Boroughs	4,286,000	
		7,125,000
(3) Counties		7,842,000
Total		£14,967,000

The Rating Question.

Hence the Rates are on Rateable Value :—

(1) Metropolis . . . . . 4s. in the £1.
(2) Cities and Boroughs . . 5s. „ „
(3) Counties . . . . . 2s. 8d. „ „

Amounts in the £1 Rateable value.

Calculated upon *Rental* they will be :—

(1) Metropolis . . . . 16 per cent.
(2) Cities and Boroughs . 20 „
(3) Counties . . . . 11 „

Percentages on Rental.

The Rates on Farms appear from many inquiries to average :

On Rateable Value . . . . 2s. in the £1.
On Rental . . . . . . 8½ per cent.

Farms.

The remainder of the County, 11 per cent., being due to the Towns within the County boundaries.

CHAPTER XIII.

THE CONSUMPTION OF CORN, TEA, COFFEE, AND SUGAR.

Chap. XIII.

BEFORE estimating the Taxes which are paid by different individuals and classes, it will be convenient to discuss the consumption of the principal articles subject to Indirect Taxation—taxes which are more nearly connected than any other with the habits and welfare of the people, and which have long been a battle-field of political strife. The amount of consumption and its growth with successive reductions of duties are worthy of attentive consideration.

Corn.

Corn is the only article of absolute necessity that pays any duty, and this more as a registration fee than as a tax. But the gradual increase of importations, as the population and its larger earnings outgrew the home production, has made the duty of some pecuniary importance, and of more dubious advisability. There is little doubt that it raises the price of corn in the British markets a shilling a quarter. The average consumption of wheat is estimated at three-fourths of a quarter per head for the poorer classes, and half a quarter among the more prosperous— making up a total consumption of about 21,000,000 quarters per annum—so that the total burden on the poor from the increase of price is about 9*d.* per head, one-third of which, or 3*d.*, is actual Taxation, and two-thirds, or 6*d.*, the indirect results of the tax. The tax on the other kinds of corn, producing an equal sum to the revenue, does not act so injuriously on the poor, affecting them chiefly through the brewers who purchase the barley. I have estimated the actual Taxation from all kinds of corn at 6*d.* per head of the population.

Tea has increased in consumption in a remarkable manner. From 1801 to 1843 the consumption per head was nearly stationary, and the increase since that time is shown in the following table :—

CONSUMPTION OF TEA—UNITED KINGDOM.

Year.	Total Consumption.	Duty.		Consumption per head.	
	lbs.	s.	d.	lbs.	oz.
1741	880,000	5	0	0	1¼
1750	2,700,000	2	0	0	4
1801	23,700,000	1	2½	1	8
1843	40,300,000	2	2¼	1	8
1852	54,700,000	2	2¼	2	0
1856	63,300,000	1	9	2	6
1867	111,000,000	0	6	3	11

CHAP. XIII.
Comparative Consumption of Tea.

Tea and Sugar Return. 184, 1857.

Statistical Abstract, 1868, p. 41.

The correspondence between the reduction of duty and the increase of consumption is very striking. The reduction from 2s. 2¼d. in 1852 to 6d. in 1867 has in fifteen years nearly doubled the consumption. In the spring of 1857 an attempt was made by the Inland Revenue Board to ascertain the consumption of the Working Classes, by returns obtained from grocers in more than 300 towns and villages in Great Britain, and a large number in Ireland. The result was an estimate which appears reliable, that at that time 56 per cent. of the consumption of tea was by the Upper and Middle Classes, and 44 per cent. by the Working Classes. As the consumption in 1856 was 63,300,000 lbs., this would give nearly 4½ lbs. per head to the Upper and Middle Classes, and 1½ lbs. per head to the Working Classes.

During the succeeding eleven years the consumption of tea has increased by 58,000,000 lbs., of which far the larger portion (probably three-fourths) has been by the working classes. After allowing for 2,000,000 increase of population, this gives an additional consumption of 1 lb. per head to the Upper and Middle Classes, and 1½ lb. per head to the Working Class. Added to the estimate of the Inland Revenue for 1856, it would make the present consumption of the Upper and Middle Classes 5½ lbs.

per head, and of the Working Classes 3 lbs. *per head*; a result which agrees pretty closely with actual inquiry.

The consumption of *Coffee* has undergone remarkable variations, shown in the following table:—

CONSUMPTION OF COFFEE—UNITED KINGDOM.

Year.	Total Consumption.	Duty per lb.		Consumption per head.	
	lbs.	s.	d.	lbs.	oz.
1740	130,000	1	6	0	½
1801	750,000	1	6	0	1
1811	6,390,000	0	7	0	8
1821	7,327,000	1	0	0	8
1841	27,300,000	0	6	1	7½
1856	35,000,000	0	4	1	4
1867	31,300,000	0	3	1	0

Porter, "Progress of the Nation," p. 549.

Hence in 1801, the high duty confined the consumption to the rich. In 1811, with a reduction to 7*d.*, the consumption had increased more than seven-fold. A rise in the duty to 1*s.* prevented any increase during the next ten years; but in 1825 the duty was reduced to 6*d.*, and, in consequence, the consumption per head in 1841 had trebled; reaching 1½lbs., its highest point. From that year it steadily declined, notwithstanding considerable reductions of duty, owing to the competition of Tea and Chicory.

The consumption of *Sugar*, like that of Tea, was

stationary from 1801 to 1843, averaging about 18 lbs. of raw Sugar per head of the population. The following table shows its subsequent increase:—

CONSUMPTION OF SUGAR—UNITED KINGDOM.

Year.	Total Consumption.	Average Duty per cwt.	Consumption per head of Raw Sugar.
	cwts.	£ s. d.	lbs.
1700	200,000	0 3 5	3
1754	1,065,000	0 6 8	12
1801 to 1814	2,850,000	1 6 2	18
1843	4,030,000	1 5 2	17
1854	8,330,000	0 11 5	34
1856	7,070,000	0 14 6	28
1867	11,700,000	0 9 4	40½

The fall in consumption in 1856, consequent on the increased duty and higher price of the Sugar itself, is remarkable. The consumption is now, with an average duty of 9s. 4d., more than double per head what it was with an average duty of 25s. 2d. in 1843.

Tea and Sugar Return, 184, 1857. The Inland Revenue collected similar reports in 1857 respecting the consumption of Sugar, and estimated from them that the Upper and Middle Classes were, in 1856, consuming 60 per cent. of the quantity sold in the shops, and the Working Classes 40 per cent. Making a reduction of 20 per cent. from the gross importation for consumption

Tea, Coffee, and Sugar. 73

by brewers and confectioners, and for loss in refining, the consumption per head would be, according to this calculation, 50 lbs. for the Upper and Middle, and 12½lbs. for the Working Classes. The increased consumption since 1856 has been enormous, amounting to 4,600,000 cwts., or, after deduction of 20 per cent. as before, 400,000,000 lbs. Allowing 50,000,000 lbs. for the increase of population, this leaves 350,000,000 lbs. to be distributed over the nation, being sufficient to give 14 lbs. per head to the Working Classes, which would raise their total to 26 lbs. *per head;* and 5 lbs. per head additional to the Upper and Middle Classes, making their consumption 55 lbs. *per head.*

It is possible to test these calculations by the results of actual inquiries. The first inquiry is contained in a paper on the Expenditure of the Working Classes of Manchester and Dukinfield in 1841, read before the British Association in that year by Mr. William Nield, Mayor of Manchester. It gives separately, in a very clear manner, the income and expenditure of eighteen families in those towns, from which I have reduced the consumption into lbs. weight, and averaged it in the following Summary:—

Statistical Abstract.

Consumption in 1841.

Journal of the Statistical Society, 1841, p. 323.

MANCHESTER AND DUKINFIELD WORKMEN, 1841.

AVERAGE OF EIGHTEEN FAMILIES.

	£	s.	d.
Income	76	0	0
Rent	9	7	9

Yearly Consumption—

	lbs. per head.
Tea	1¼
Coffee	3
Sugar	17½
Tobacco	9½ ozs.

Beer and Spirits not accounted for.

The duties at this time were—Tea 2s. 2½d. and Coffee 6d. per lb.; Sugar, 25s. 2d. per cwt. and Tobacco 3s. per lb. It must be borne in mind that Manchester has the highest scale of consumption in the kingdom, so that this is the most favourable specimen that could be selected for 1841.

Consumption in 1861. Mr. Macdonald. The next inquiry was in 1861, recorded in a pamphlet published by Mr. Francis Macdonald, giving the consumption of 6,150 families for three months of that year at Manchester, Rochdale, and Bacup, as shown by the books of the Co-operative Stores. I am told at Rochdale that these returns have a tendency to be in excess of the working class expenditure, from the tickets often falling into the hands of the class above them. I have reduced the totals to the average per head in the following Summary:—

Tea, Coffee, and Sugar.

CONSUMPTION AT MANCHESTER, ROCHDALE, AND BACUP, 1861. AVERAGE OF 6,150 FAMILIES.

Yearly Consumption—

	lbs. per head.
Tea	2
Coffee	2½
Sugar	50
Tobacco	1⅓

The duty on Tea had then fallen to 1s. 5d. and on Coffee to 3d. per lb., and upon Sugar to 14s. per cwt.; Tobacco remaining the same. The amount of Sugar appears rather large, although accounted for by a Manchester consumption.

A third inquiry has been made by myself, at Christmas 1868, by the aid of correspondents in many different parts of the country, whom I have to thank for very valuable information. Returns were sent to me from large houses, and by gentlemen, tradesmen, and clerks, of every class of income, which I have summarized in the following Table:— *Consumption in 1868. Upper and Middle Classes.*

CONSUMPTION OF THE UPPER AND MIDDLE CLASSES, 1868.

Article.	Large Houses. per head.	Upper Middle Class. per head.	Lower Middle Class. per head.	Average being nearer the most numerous Class.
	lbs.	lbs.	lbs.	lbs.
Tea	12 to 10	11 to 5	5 to 2½	5½
Sugar	100 to 90	70 to 50	50 to 26	50

Coffee—very irregular, but where drunk it is in much the same quantities as Tea.

CHAP. XIII.
Working Classes.

Numerous returns were also sent to me of the Consumption of the Working Classes, both in London and the Country, by clergymen and tradesmen (especially grocers) who had opportunities of obtaining accurate information, and could speak to the average consumption in their localities. These returns are classified in the following Summary:—

CONSUMPTION OF WORKING MEN, 1868.

ARTICLES.	1. Families in Central London, St. George's-in-the-East, Poplar, and Chelsea.	2. Manufacturing Families in Manchester, Rochdale, Sheffield, and Wakefield.	3. Families in Country Towns, Doncaster, and Hastings.	4. Farm Labourers in Yorkshire, Dorset, and Sussex.
	lbs. per head.	lbs. per head.	lbs. per head.	lbs. per head.
Tea	5	5	3¼	2
Coffee	7	4	2	—
Sugar	41	45	28	16
Tobacco	1¼	1½	1	⅘

The Duties were 6d. per lb. of tea, and 3d. for coffee; 9s. 4d. per cwt. average for sugar, and 3s. 2d. per lb. for tobacco.

Comparing Column 2 of this Table with the Summaries for 1841 and 1861, it is easy to see the progress that has been made.

The Average must be taken nearer the lowest and most numerous class.

AVERAGE WORKING CLASS CONSUMPTION, 1868.

	lbs. per head.
Tea	3
Coffee	1
Sugar	25
Tobacco	1

Such are the dry figures, but when we consider their real meaning, how great is their importance! Every individual of the working classes now consumes on the average 3 lbs. of tea during the year, in the place of *one* in 1841, and of *one and a hal* in 1857; making every meal more cheering and comfortable, and promoting sobriety. Every child of a working-class family now gets on the average twice as much sugar as in 1857, to supply the deficiencies of a scanty diet. The upper classes would not like to be deprived of their tea, but to them it is a luxury of life. "With working people," says an Edinburgh correspondent, "tea and coffee are more articles of food than with those who have plenty of food without them." They drink them three times a day—for breakfast, dinner, and tea, though weaker than we should be satisfied with,—the cheapest and readiest, and, next to milk, most wholesome accompaniment of a meal. An old woman, with half-a-crown and a loaf a week from the parish, spends $2\frac{1}{2}d.$ in tea (being at the rate of 3 lbs. a year), the only stimulant she can afford. Irish families in Connemara, who seldom taste meat, are great consumers of tea and sugar, eating the sugar upon their bread and in their stirabout in large quantities as often as they can get it. The underpaid and highly-rented poor at the East End of London

CHAP.
XIII.

depend almost as much upon the same articles. Thus from Land's End to John o' Groats, and from the Giant's Causeway to the rock of Valentia, the whole population of the three kingdoms has been benefited by the reduction of the Taxes upon Tea and Sugar.

POPULATION OF THE UNITED KINGDOM.

The following Table of Population may be useful for the Tables which precede and follow :—

Year.	England and Wales.	Scotland.	Ireland.	United Kingdom.
1700	5,130,000	—	—	—
1750	6,040,000	1,260,000	2,370,000	9,670,000
1801	9,060,000	1,625,000	5,215,000	15,900,000
1821	12,100,000	2,100,000	6,800,000	21,000,000
1841	15,930,000	2,620,000	8,200,000	26,750,000
1861	20,120,000	3,067,000	5,788,000	28,975,000
1867	21,430,000	3,170,000	5,557,000	30,157,000

CHAPTER XIV.

THE CONSUMPTION OF TOBACCO AND ALCOHOL.

TOBACCO is often said to be taken by the poorest classes as a substitute for food. But, from whatever cause, so great are its attractions, that the Taxation voluntarily paid by the five and a half million adult males of the Manual Labour Classes for its consumption amounts to an average Poll Tax of 15s. each. This represents $4\frac{3}{4}$lbs. a year, or $1\frac{1}{2}$ oz. per week, which is considered a moderate family allowance. The amount varies from 1 oz. a week with the agricultural labourer or poor mechanic, up to 4 or even 6 ozs. a week with constant smokers among the well-paid artisans. Men who work for themselves, as at Sheffield, or follow intermittent occupations, like fishermen, are the greatest smokers. Those who work under superintendence are the least. In some places, as at Sheffield, the wives frequently share their husbands' tobacco, and smoke

CHAP. XIV. Tobacco.

See also Appendix III., Table 6, as to Wakefield.

from 2 to 3 ozs. per week. I am told that about three-fourths of the working men smoke, and that 2 ozs. per week is the commonest scale of consumption. The total consumption by all classes is as follows:—

CONSUMPTION OF TOBACCO—UNITED KINGDOM.

See Porter's "Progress of the Nation," p. 565. and Statistical Abstract, pp. 41, 42.

Year.	Total Consumption.	Average Duty per lb.		Consumption per head.	
	lbs.	s.	d.	lbs.	ozs.
1789	10,900,000	1	0	0	12
1801	16,900,000	1	7	1	0
1821	15,600,000	4	0	0	12
1841	22,300,000	3	0	0	13
1860	35,200,000	3	2	1	4
1867	40,800,000	3	2	1	$5\frac{1}{3}$

Thus the habit of smoking was checked in the first twenty years of the present century by the duty being nearly trebled. It remained stationary during the next twenty years, notwithstanding a reduction of the duty. It has increased nearly 50 per cent. during the last twenty-seven years, while the duty has been slightly raised, an increase due to the prosperity and larger earnings of the nation.

Wine. *Wine* is still a luxury of the Upper and Middle Classes; and even by them is sparingly used by those whose income is under £600 or £700 a-year. This is to a great extent the effect of Taxation,

Consumption of Wine.—United Kingdom.

Year.	Total Consumption.	Average Duty.		Consumption per head.
	Gallons.	s.	d.	Gallons.
England & Wales.				
1669	11,000,000	0	4	2·5
1700	5,600,000	2	2	1·1
1750	4,000,000	5	0	·7
United Kingdom.				
1801	6,900,000	6	3	·43
1821	4,700,000	8	5	·22
1841	6,200,000	5	5	·23
1859	6,770,000	5	2	·23
1867	13,670,000	2	0	·42

Commons' Committee on Wine Duties, 1852, pp. 163, 518.

Porter, "Progress of the Nation," p. 560.

Statistical Abstract, 1857, pp. 41, 42.

since in the sixteenth century the consumption was many times as great per head of the population.

Observe the reduction in a century and a half from two and a half gallons per head to one-tenth of the amount, and the doubled consumption during the last eight years in consequence of the lowering of the duty. The consumption of Wine in France was stated, in 1851, by Mr. Porter, to be 19 gallons per head. But this more properly corresponds with the consumption of beer in the United Kingdom, which, in 1867, was 29 gallons per head.

An estimate of the consumption of Wine by persons of different incomes will be found in the Appendix, showing an average expenditure of 5 (Appendix II. Table 2.)

82   Consumption of Tobacco and Alcohol.

CHAP. XIV.

per cent., and duty paid of 10s. per cent. for Wine, on incomes above £500 a year.

Beer and Porter.

Beer and Porter are taxed by the Malt Duty of 2s. 8½d., and by a License Duty on Brewers of 3½d. per bushel (which was imposed as a substitute for the Hop Duty), bringing up the total Tax to 3s. per bushel. From 1697 to 1830 there was also a Beer Tax which was only paid by the public Brewers, and not by private brewings, which at that time were far more common than at present. This Duty was complicated and continually varied, but may roughly be stated as follows:—

Malt Tax Report, 1867, Evidence, Q. 182.

Do. Appendix III.

AVERAGE BEER TAX PER GALLON, 1697 TO 1830.

1697 to 1757, Strong Beer 2d., Small Beer ½d.
1758 to 1800, Strong Beer 3d., Small Beer ½d.
1801 to 1830, Strong Beer nearly 4d., Small Beer ⅝d.

It constituted a most oppressive Tax on the Brewers, and — judging from the quantity of Malt — it appears to have been paid by about half the total quantity brewed. It was repealed in 1830.

Consumption in England and Wales.

The following table shows the consumption in England and Wales since 1700. A bushel of Malt is estimated to produce on an average 18 gallons of Beer, but, in order to avoid an excessive calculation, I have estimated the produce per bushel as, 14 gallons per bushel in 1706, 15 gallons in 1750, 17 gallons 1803 to 1830, and afterwards at 18 gallons.

CONSUMPTION OF MALT, BEER, AND PORTER.   CHAP. XIV.

ENGLAND AND WALES.

Year. England and Wales.	Total Consumption.		Average Duty.		Consumption per Head.
	Malt.	Beer.	s.	d.	
	Bushels.	Gallons.			Galls. of Beer.
1706	23,000,000	325,000,000	0	6¾	62
1750	29,000,000	435,000,000	0	6¾	72
1803	29,560,000	502,500,000	2	5	55
1821	26,130,000	444,300,000	3	7¼	37
1830	26,900,000	457,300,000	2	7	33
1841	30,950,000	557,100,000	2	8½	35
1861	39,200,000	706,000,000	2	0	35
1867	42,150,000	758,000,000	2	8½	36

It is important to notice the increase from 1706 to 1730, and the decrease from 1750 to 1830, when for eighty years the total consumption of Malt remained stationary with an increasing population, and the consumption per head diminished to less than half. Since 1830 there has been a large increase in the total quantity of Malt, but only a small increase in the quantity of Beer per head.

The Beer exported, corresponding to 1,000,000 bushels of Malt in 1867, and 750,000 in 1861, is deducted in both those years. I have not been able to find a previous account, but it was probably not important in 1841.

CHAP. XIV.
Scotland and Ireland.

The consumption in Scotland and Ireland is given in the same Return.

CONSUMPTION OF BEER IN SCOTLAND AND IRELAND, 1867.

Country.	Malt.	Year.	Malt Duty Average.	Consumption per Head.
	Bushels.	Gallons.	s. d.	Gallons.
Scotland .	2,360,000	42,500,000	2 5	14
Ireland .	2,370,000	42,700,000	2 5	7½

These figures exclude the quantity sent into other parts of the United Kingdom or exported. Hence the consumption of Beer in Scotland is only two-fifths, and in Ireland one-fifth, of the consumption in England. In both Scotland and Ireland the Beer is drunk almost exclusively by the Upper and Middle Classes. An Irish correspondent says, "The poor would think as little of it, if given them, as they would of Mr. Gladstone's cheap Claret!"

Spirits.

Spirits are now taxed as highly as at any period of our history. The Excise duties on British Spirits began in 1660, with 2*d.* and 3*d.* per gallon.

Inland Revenue, First Report, Appendix, p. 41.

The consumption in England and Wales gradually increased from 527,000 gallons in 1684, to 1,675,000 gallons in 1706, and to 6,000,000 gallons paying duty in 1736. The increase of drunkenness occasioned the greatest apprehensions, and gave rise to continual debates in Parliament. It had become the practice of some publicans to entice customers by a notice painted on boards outside their houses to this effect:—"You may here get drunk for a penny, dead drunk for twopence, and have clean straw for nothing."

The Gin Act was passed in 1736, imposing a duty of 20s. per gallon, and prohibiting sale by retail under very heavy penalties. Riots and violence followed, the clandestine sale of gin was continued, and the prisons were filled with offenders. The Act became a dead letter. In 1742 it had to be repealed, and moderate duties substituted. In 1743 it was stated in evidence before a Committee of the House of Commons that the quantity of spirituous liquors consumed in England and Wales had gradually risen from 10,000,000 gallons in 1733, to 19,000,000 gallons in 1742, of which 11,000,000 were the produce of illicit distillation. These quantities were consumed by a population of six millions, giving in the latter year more than three gallons of spirits per head. It was a common thing to see numbers of men and women rolling about the streets drunk. Nor were habits of drunkenness confined to the labouring classes.

The Duties were gradually increased from 1743

to the end of the century, and acquired a very complicated character. The three kingdoms had each a different scale, both for home-made, for foreign, and for colonial spirits. In the table for the United Kingdom which follows, the average is taken from the total payments.

CONSUMPTION OF SPIRITS.—UNITED KINGDOM.

Spirits and Malt Return, 1868.

Year.	Total Consumption.	Average Duty.	Consumption per head.
	gallons.	s. d.	gallons.
1802	15,600,000	6 1	·98
1821	13,160,000	10 4	·63
1841	24,100,000	6 2	·90
1859	28,660,000	8, 4	·80
1867	29,530,000	10 1	·98

It would appear from these figures that the consumption of the United Kingdom is now the same per head as in the beginning of the century. But the prevalence of illicit distillation is an important and disturbing element in the calculation. It was probably much larger in Scotland and Ireland in the beginning of the century than at present. The Revenue Commissioners, in their fifth Report, state that in 1811, with a duty of 2s. 6d. a gallon, duty was paid in Ireland on 6,500,000 gallons; and that in 1822, when the duty was raised to 5s. 6d., only

2,900,000 gallons paid duty, when the total Irish consumption was 10,000,000 gallons per annum, thus leaving 7,000,000 gallons for illicit production. The suppression of this traffic was found to be impossible, and the attempt led to the greatest popular exasperation and disorganization. On the reduction of the duty to 2s. 4d., the quantity paying duty in Ireland rose by degrees to 12,300,000 gallons in 1838. Since that year it has steadily declined, at first owing to the influence of Father Mathew, but more permanently with the advance of the duty. It was only 4,700,000 gallons in 1859, with an 8s. duty, and now stands at 4,900,000 gallons, with a 10s. duty.

The following table shows the distribution of Spirit Consumption between the three kingdoms:—

CONSUMPTION OF SPIRITS, 1867.
ENGLAND, SCOTLAND, IRELAND.

Country.	British, Foreign, and Colonial.	Average Duty.		Consumption per head.	Spirits and Malt Return, 1868.
	Gallons.	s.	d.	Gallons.	
England and Wales	18,486,000	10	1	·9	
Scotland	5,800,000	10	0	2·0	
Ireland	5,248,000	10	0	·93	

These purport to be the quantities actually consumed in each country, after deducting the quantity exported or removed from one part of the kingdom to another. The 10,000,000 gallons consumed in Ireland in 1811, by a population less by half a million than the present, and the 12,000,000 gallons consumed in 1838 by a population two and a quarter millions greater than the present number, together with the present high duty, makes me fear that the real consumption of Spirits in Ireland is very largely in excess of that which pays duty, and that it will be at least a gallon and a half per head. It seems incredible that the Irish consumption of alcoholic drinks by the working classes should be less than the English by the whole amount of the staple drink in England —the Beer.

Increase of Temperance. These tables furnish some interesting deductions as to the progress of temperance. The consumption of alcoholic liquors in England and Wales appears to have been as follows:—

CONSUMPTION PER HEAD OF ALCOHOLIC DRINKS.
ENGLAND AND WALES.

Year.	Wine.	Spirits.	Beer.
	Gall.	Gall.	Gall.
1700 to 1706 .	1·1	·33	62·
1743 to 1750 .	·7	3·	72·
1802 to 1806 .	·43	·9	55·
1867	·42	·9	36·

Hence two results. *First*, that, on the average of the whole population, the consumption of the nineteenth century is only half that of the eighteenth. *Second*, that, notwithstanding the immense increase of prosperity and earnings— a very powerful element in alcoholic expenditure —the consumption of Wine and Spirits in 1867 is the same as in 1802; while the consumption of Beer (notwithstanding the rally in 1830) is reduced 44 per cent. Thus, two great steps have been gained during the last 150 years in the diminution of intemperance.

The expenditure of temperate men on alcoholic drinks varies very much in proportion to their income. That of the intemperate is only bounded by their income. The following particulars of the habits of different classes derived from informants of great experience may be interesting:—

Present distribution of consumption.

ENGLISH WORKMEN.

1. A temperate *Agricultural Labourer*, with £45 or £50 a year will take one glass or two glasses a day, amounting, with occasional additions, to 25 or 50 gallons per family per annum. He scarcely ever tastes spirits, and his wife has only an occasional glass of beer, unless nursing.

England and Wales. Working-men. Temperate.

2. A temperate *Town Workman*, with £50 to £60 a year, will with his wife take three glasses a day (1¼ pints), or (including occasional additions) 75 gallons per family per year; drinking occasionally spirits, say one or at most two gallons per family per year. This will be an expenditure of 2*s*. or 2*s*. 6*d*. a week, and is in addition to 6*d*. or 1*s*. on tobacco.

CHAP. XIV.

3. A temperate *Artisan*, with 35s. to 40s. a week, will drink, with his family, 3 pints (or 6 glasses) of beer per diem, say 150 gallons per family per year, and 1 to 2 quarterns of spirits a week, or 2 to 4 gallons a year. This will represent an expenditure of 4s. 6d. to 5s. a week, and is commonly in addition to 1s. per week for tobacco.

All the above quantities are *per family*, and require division by 4 or 5 to obtain the quantity *per head*.

Intemperate.

4. *Intemperate, or excessive expenditures,* are far beyond this scale. Half the wages to the man for beer, spirits, and tobacco, and the other half to the wife for the rent, and " to do for" the family, is reported by many correspondents as not unusual. The Irish spend more than the English in proportion to their earnings; but with both English and Irish the Saturday night drinking often exhausts the week's wages. And sittings of two or three days' duration, which are sadly too frequent in some localities, make away with considerable savings.

ENGLISH MIDDLE CLASSES.

Middle Classes.

5. Careful families with £100 a year,—and clerks of that income are obliged to be far more careful than working men of the same means, since they have more appearance to keep up—seem from my returns to consume about 25 gallons of beer *per head*, and 2 to 3 gallons of spirits per annum.

6. In families of small incomes, where women servants only are kept, 35 to 40 gallons *per head* of beer are drunk. The Spirits are very small, and Wine begins to come in.

UPPER CLASSES.

Upper Classes.

7. In families with large incomes, where there are men servants and visiting—a very much smaller number than is commonly supposed—the quantity of beer ranges from 50 to 100 gallons *per head*. The consumption of spirits is not large.

All the above statements are in Spirits of the strength usually sold, which for the Upper Classes is usually 10 per cent. below proof, and for the Working Classes 25 per cent. below proof.

Twenty-five per cent. below proof means, that out of 100 parts of the mixture 25 are water and 75 spirit, so adding *one-third* to the total quantity of proof spirit. Thus, if the temperate consumption of the Working Classes is 16,000,000 gallons of proof spirits, this represents at least 21,200,000 gallons of diluted spirit, as sold to them over the counter. This addition must always be borne in mind in reckoning their taxation, since the diluted spirit has paid 7s. 6d. per gallon duty instead of 10s.

On the whole, I should estimate the *temperate expenditure* in England, as:—Upper and Middle Classes, 35 gallons of Beer per head; half a gallon of diluted Spirits. Manual Labour Classes, 20 gallons of Beer per head; half a gallon of diluted Spirits.

In Scotland more than half of the beer, and in Ireland almost the whole of it, must be attributed to the Upper and Middle Classes; and most of the duty-paying Spirits may be distributed over the population, estimated at two gallons per head of diluted spirit in Scotland, and nine-tenths of a gallon in Ireland. This leaves the intemperate consumption to be supplied by the balance and by illicit distillation.

The Upper and Middle Classes in both those countries drink much less Wine and more Spirits than in England.

We can now proceed to calculate the relative Taxation of the different classes of the community.

CHAPTER XV.

TAXES ON PROPERTY AND INCOME.

Chap. XV.
The Income Tax.

THE Income Tax is an excellent example of the love of the British nation for abstract principles. It is founded upon two — the great principle of Direct Taxation, so strongly advocated by Financial Reformers; and the still greater principle of Equality of Taxation, so dear to Political Economists. Yet, if the Income Tax should be the test, it will be difficult to decide which of the twain is the most cordially hated by a discerning public. Two incidents may show the current of popular feeling. In his Budget-speech of 1860, which re-imposed the Income Tax, Mr. Gladstone related that he had received, about a fortnight before, a letter addressed to him, complaining of the monstrous injustice and iniquity of the Income Tax, and proposing that, in consideration thereof, the Chancellor of the Exchequer

Taxes on Property and Income. 93

should be publicly hanged! In the newspapers a few weeks ago appeared a police report, chronicling the adventures and punishment of a couple of ingenious gentlemen, who contrived for some time to make a good living out of the squires and inhabitants of some Warwickshire villages by petitions and collecting books, which purported to emanate from an Anti-Income Tax Association!

CHAP. XV.

The very equality of the tax is held to prove its inequality. But true equalization is an insoluble problem. The complaints are reducible under two principal heads :—

Objections to the Income Tax.

1. That it is unjust to tax Interests for Life or Years at the same per centage as Absolute Interests.

2. That it is unjust to tax Incomes from Land, Personalty and Industry at the same total rate of assessment.

But the principles involved in these objections have a far wider range than the Income Tax. They affect our whole system of Taxation, and, if just and sound, ought to be adopted as its fundamental basis. Let us consider them with the care that is due to their importance.

1. As regards the different kinds of Interests, it is very curious to observe the infinite variety that prevails in every kind of Property. Scarcely

Interests in Property and Income.

two possessors of Realty, or Personalty, or Income, have exactly the same interest. One has the absolute ownership, another is proprietor for life, a third for years, a fourth has invested his capital in an annuity, a fifth holds it until some contingency, and a sixth (as a clergyman) during the performance of certain duties. All these interests may be complicated, by mortgages, in an infinite variety. All but the first will differ among themselves according to the age of the Life occupant or the years unexpired of the Lease. Not only are they various, but they shade off into each other with almost imperceptible gradations. The highest of an inferior class of interests are superior in permanency and value to the lowest of the higher grade. The following Table shows more clearly their variety, excluding of course Reversionary Interests :—

POSSESSORY INTERESTS IN PROPERTY OR INCOME.

I. *In Land*—
 (a) The Estate in Fee.
 (b) The Leasehold, with from one to 1,000 years' duration.
 (c) The Life Estate, with from one to seventy years' probability of Life, or till some contingency.

II. *In Personalty*—
 (d) The absolute property.
 (e) The Life Estate as before.
 (f) The Annuity, with similar probability of life; but in which capital is yearly vanishing.

III. *Industrial Incomes*—

(*y*) Businesses which are family property.
(*h*) Professions or appointments which are virtually for life.
(*k*) Employments of precarious duration.

Ought these interests to be capitalized, and the taxes to be paid on the capitalized value? It would require the most complicated rules and calculations, far beyond the power of ordinary tax-collectors, and practicably unworkable. We should want Actuaries for tax-gatherers. Besides, as Mr. Mill points out, if the life-income is to be capitalized, the life-taxes must be capitalized also, which will bring them back to the same percentage as on permanent property. Political Economy, Book v. s. 4.

But an impracticable scheme is seldom right in principle. The more simple view is that the Taxes for the year protect the property or income for the year, and must be paid by the occupant for the time being, in proportion to the yearly assessable value of the property occupied. The Taxpayer is the tenant of the house, perhaps as absolute owner, perhaps for life, perhaps for years; but in either case he is bound to maintain and defend it, and hand it down in the same state to his successor. In no case is he entitled to call upon his neighbour to contribute towards the obliga-

CHAP. XV

Land, Personalty, and Industry.

tion. I apprehend that this is the right and practical view of Taxation, and the one which is adopted and carried out by English Law.

2. Thus in almost all Taxes on Income and Property, whether Land Tax, Probate Duty, Legacy Duty, or Income Tax, the State makes—and finds itself practically obliged to make—no distinction in respect of length or shortness of interest, but assesses the holder of the Income for the time being at the full rate. For similar reasons it would be inconvenient to make a distinction in any one Tax, so as to assess Landed Income at one rate, Personalty at another rate, and Industry at a third, as advocated for the Income Tax. Nor is it necessary; because these different classes of Income are subject for the most part to different taxes, as Land Tax and Rates on Land, and Probate and Legacy Duty on Personalty, and their total taxation is very different. Let us see what in justice ought to be the amount of this difference.

Land.

Land, which is the best kind of investment, produces a smaller income in proportion to its value than *Personalty*, and, if its total taxes amounted to the same income-percentage, would escape at a lighter rate. Hence the total taxes on Land ought to amount to a larger percentage on its annual value than on Personalty. A Landed

Taxes on Property and Income.

family choose the smaller return for their Capital, because land is a growing property and confers dignity and consequence. But that is no reason why they should be more lightly taxed. Land produces a gross income of $3\frac{1}{3}$ per cent. before deduction of Rates. It ought in justice to pay the same taxes as if it produced 4 per cent. like the best kinds of personalty. But this is an increase of one-fifth. So that a Landed Income ought to pay a percentage of taxes *one-fifth higher* than the percentage on Incomes from Personalty.

Personalty may be taken as the standard.

Industrial Incomes, being precarious in their nature, are entitled to a lower total of taxes, in order to allow for Savings and Insurance, and this allowance is fairly put by Mr. Mill at one-fourth.

> To give an example, a man with £500 a year from business would consider his family well provided for at his death by an Insurance or Savings producing £250 a year, that is to say, by a Capital of £6,000. This amount, insured on a good life, and commencing at 26 years of age, will cost in premiums about £125 a year, or one-fourth of his income. Savings (which avoid the stamp duty, expenses and profit of the Insurance Company) ought, on an average length of life, to produce the same capital from a less annual sum. Hence *one-fourth* is a fair allowance of exemption for an Industrial Income.

It follows that an Industrial Income ought to bear a percentage of Taxes *one-fourth lower* than that of Personalty.

Taxes on Property and Income.

CHAP. XV.
Normal Proportions of Taxation.

Hence the relative proportions of total Taxation to Income of these three great divisions ought to be:—

Landed Incomes	$1\frac{1}{8}$
Personalty Incomes	1
Industrial Incomes	$\frac{3}{4}$

Thus, if the total Taxation on Personalty is 7 per cent., the Taxation on the three divisions should be—

Landed Incomes	$8\frac{1}{2}$ per cent.
Personalty Incomes	7 ,,
Industrial Incomes	5 ,,

Or, if the total Taxation on Personalty is found to be 12 per cent., the proportions should be—

Landed Incomes	$14\frac{1}{2}$ per cent.
Personalty Incomes	12 ,,
Industrial Incomes	9 ,,

Let us see how far the principle of distinction between these three classes of Income is carried in the Taxation of the United Kingdom.

Total Taxes on Income.
The following are the Taxes which fall upon each.

From Land.

I. TAXES ON INCOME FROM LAND.

	Per Cent.
See p. 26. 1. *Property Tax*, at 5d. in the £1 (the amount in 1867)	2
2. *Land Tax*, which is very irregular in amount, but averages	1
Page 29. 3. *Succession Duty*, the interest on the amount paid, averaging	$1\frac{1}{2}$
Page 26. 4. *Stamps on Deeds and Law Fees*, which together average nearly	$\frac{1}{2}$
See Chap. XII. Pages 62 and 67. 5. *Local Rates*, the three-fourths which fall on the landlord, averaging on the rent of a farm	6
Total taxes per cent.	11

Thus the Taxes on Income of Real Property, without any addition from taxes on Expenditure, amount to £11 per £100 of Rent; with the usual deductions for Income Tax if under £200.

II. TAXES ON INCOME FROM PERSONALTY.

	Per Cent.	
1. *Property Tax*, at 5d. in the £1	2	From Personalty
2. *Probate Duty*, interest on the amount paid, averaging	2	See p. 28.
3. *Legacy Duty*, ditto	2½	
(Succession duty is paid if the property passes by Settlement.)		
4. *Stamps and Law Fees*, averaging	½	
Total taxes per cent.	7	

Thus the Taxes on Income from Personalty (except Leaseholds and Railway Shares), and without any addition from Taxes on Expenditure, amount to £7 per £100, or less than *two-thirds* of those on Income from Real Property.

III. TAXES ON INDUSTRIAL INCOMES.

	Per Cent.	
1. *Income Tax*, at 5d. in the £1	2	Industrial Incomes.
2. *Stamps and Law Fees*, averaging	½	
3. *Taxes on Professions and Trades* (not recovered from the Public), averaging	1	See p. 35.
Total taxes per cent.	3½	

Hence the total actual Taxes on Income from these three classes are (if above £100)— Comparison of Taxation

Real Property Incomes	11 per cent.
Personalty ,,	7 ,,
Industrial ,,	3½ ,,

Thus, so far as Taxes on Income are concerned, Industrial Incomes pay only *half* the taxation paid by Personalty Incomes, and only *one-third* the taxation paid by Real Property Incomes.

These proportions, compared with those stated on the preceding page, show that Landed Incomes are taxed 2½ per cent. in excess of the normal standard, and Industrial Incomes 1½ per cent. below it. Hence also it is clear, that those who agitate for a more stringent Succession Duty on Real Property, on the ground of its being more lightly taxed than Personalty, do so in ignorance of the real facts of the case, since Real Property is much more heavily taxed than Personalty.

CHAPTER XVI.

TAXES ON TRADES AND PROFESSIONS, AND CONVEYANCE.

THESE Taxes are relics of the Dark Ages, when nothing could be done without the permission of the Crown. They are very partial in their operation, taxing some employments and leaving others untaxed. In the taxed employments they are unequal upon individuals, falling heavily on poor men with small business and lightly upon rich men with large. The least objectionable might appear to be those on the sale of alcoholic drinks and tobacco, which fall upon the consumer and raise the price of the articles supplied, so restricting the sale. But it is a question whether a greater portion of this increase does not go into the pocket of the retailer, and less into the Exchequer, than if the increase had been caused by a higher duty on the articles themselves.

Licences on Trades and Professions.

CHAP. XVI.
Beer and Spirit Licences.

The Licence Duties on Beer raise the 5s. 5d. duty on Malt to 6s. per barrel of 36 gallons, or 2d. per gallon. Those on Spirits raise the price about 5 per cent., and may be taken as a set-off against the excess of reduction below 25 per cent. under proof, which is customary with retail spirit-sellers.

Hackney Carriage Duties.

One of the most oppressive duties is that on Cabs, of which I have been furnished with the following details :—*

TAXES ON CABS.

	£
The income from a cab and two horses is 10s. per day, or per year	182
Deduct—	
Expenses of keep, 42s. per week . £109	
Renewals and repairs 8	
Interest on £100 capital . . . 5	
——	122
Net Profit	£60
The taxes on this profit are—	
Stamp-Office Plate £1	
Duty, 1s. per day, or 18	
—	£19

being an Income Tax of 32 *per cent.*, or more than 6s. in the pound. It cannot be urged that this is a tax on the public, since the fare of 6d. per mile, fixed by law, is below the usual charge for hired carriages.

Railway Shareholders.

The case of Railways is one of peculiar hardship. They are liable to the Local Rates on Real Property and to the Probate and Legacy Duties on Personalty, and have besides to pay the Government duty, inherited from the stage carriages which they superseded. These taxes will be as follows, omitting all mention of stamps.

TAXES ON RAILWAY PROPERTY.

	Per Cent.
1. Property Tax, at 5d.	2
2. Probate Duty, interest on amount paid	2
3. Legacy Duty „ „	2½
4. Rates and Taxes, averaging	4⅓
5. Government Duty	2½
Total	13⅓

This is nearly twice as high a Taxation as that paid by other Personalty, and therefore unjust. But it is made much higher by the necessary constitution of Railway Capital. The Railway Capital of 1867 was :—

	£
Debenture bonds and stock	126,000,000
Preference shares and stock	143,000,000
Ordinary „ „	233,600,000
Total	£502,000,000

The Net Revenue, 1867, was £19,600,000, which was thus appropriated :—

	Interest on Dividend.	
	Per Cent.	Total.
		£
Debenture Capital	4½	5,670,000
Preference „	4¾	6,860,000
Ordinary „	3	7,070,000
	4	£19,600,000

104   *Taxes on Trades, Professions, &c.*

The Rates and Government Duty were :—

	£	£
Rates	853,000	
Government Duty	477,000	
Total .	———	1,330,000

But the Debentures and Preference Capital receive their interest and dividends without any deduction except Property Tax, so that the whole weight of the rates and duty falls upon Ordinary Shareholders. It is equivalent to a Taxation of £1,330,000 paid out of a gross fund of £8,400,000, or nearly 16 per cent., besides Income Tax and the Probate and Legacy Duties.

Hence the Taxation on *Ordinary Shares and Stock* in Railway Companies cannot be less than 22 *per cent.* on the average Profits accruing to them from their business as Carriers. This is the rate on Companies of average prosperity. It is less per cent. on those whose prosperity is above the average; but on distressed Companies it rises to 40, 80, and even 100 per cent., and becomes confiscation of the property of Ordinary Shareholders. Considering the benefits conferred on the nation by Railway enterprise, in the immense increase of Trade and of the value of Property, this is a hardship which ought to be lessened or removed.

CHAPTER XVII.

TAXES ON EXPENDITURE.

EXPENDITURE varies with the caprice of the individual, as well as with the amount of his income, so that it is impossible to estimate with precision what the Taxation upon it will be. But, at the same time, a certain scale of expenditure is usual in each scale of income; and, by taking examples of the average expenditure in each class of the community, we may arrive at an approximate estimate of the amount of taxes they are likely to pay. *Chap. XVII.*

In the Upper and Middle Classes I propose to take three such examples,—one from the Wealthy Class, a second from the Upper Middle, and the third from the Lower Middle Class. *Upper and Middle Classes.*

1. The family of a wealthy man of £5,000 a-year. Such a family might have a town house as well as a country house, worth, to rent, £400 and £150.

They might have an indoor establishment of two men servants and seven women, besides half a dozen outdoor men as grooms, gardeners, and gamekeepers, with horses and carriages in proportion.

2. The family of a professional man or tradesman with £500 a-year. They might live in a house at £50 rent, and keep three women servants.

3. The family of a clerk with £99 a-year salary, living without any servant in a house at £15 a-year rent.

The family in each case may be supposed to consist of the father and mother and three children.

The Taxes on the house and establishment will be—

1. *The Rates*, of which the tenant's half will average 8 per cent. on the rent;
2. *The Assessed Taxes*, which, including the House Duty of 9d. in the £1 on the two first incomes, average a little more than one-half per cent. on those incomes;
3. *The Plate, Game, and Dog Licenses*, which belong almost exclusively to large incomes;
4. *The Fire Insurance Duties*, averaging 1½ per cent. on the rent; and
5. *Receipt Stamps, Drafts, Tolls*, and part of the *Postage Stamps*, averaging 1 per cent. on the income.

The whole Taxes on expenditure will be—

Taxes on Expenditure.

UPPER AND MIDDLE CLASSES.

	1. £5000 a year.			2. £500 a year.			3. £99 a year.		
I. Houses and Establishments—	£	s.	d.	£	s.	d.	£	s.	d.
Rates (Tenant's half)	44	0	0	5	0	0	1	15	0
Assessed Taxes	43	0	0	3	0	0	—		
Plate, Game, and Dogs	15	0	0	—			—		
Fire Insurance	8	0	0	1	0	0	—		
Receipts, Stamps, Tolls, &c.	50	0	0	5	0	0	0	15	0
	£160	0	0	£14	0	0	£2	10	0
II. Corn, Tea, &c.—									
Corn	0	7	0	0	4	0	0	2	6
Tea	3	10	0	1	4	0	0	10	0
Coffee	1	8	0	0	8	0	0	5	0
Sugar	5	5	0	1	13	4	0	19	0
Fruits	2	0	0	0	10	8	0	2	6
	£12	10	0	£4	0	0	£1	19	0
III. Alcohol & Tobacco—									
Tobacco	6	12	0	2	10	0	1	2	0
Wine	26	0	0	1	12	0	—		
Beer	9	10	0	2	11	0	1	2	0
Spirits	5	8	0	1	2	0	1	1	0
	£47	10	0	£7	15	0	£3	5	0
Total	£220	0	0	£25	15	0	£7	14	0
Per centage on Income	4·5			5·1			7·8		

In the above Table the following consumption is assumed for the three classes of incomes; on the estimates at pages 75, 90, and Appendix II.:—

Tea, 10 lbs., 6 lbs., and 4 lbs. per head. *Coffee*, 8 lbs., 4 lbs., and 4 lbs. per head.

Sugar, 90 lbs., 50 lbs., and 45 lbs. per head. *Tobacco*, 3 lbs., 2 lbs., and 1½ lbs. per head. *Beer*, 80 galls., 40 galls., and 25 galls. per head.

Spirits, 12 galls., 2½ galls., and 2½ galls. per family. *Wine*, 130 doz., 8 doz. per family.

CHAP. XVII.

Objections have been made to counting the taxes on servants' tea, sugar, and beer, as Taxation of their masters, because allowances are often given for those articles. But the amount which this would deduct is small and very uncertain, and does not affect the main result. The allowances would probably be diminished, if prices were much diminished, and it is on the whole safer and more simple to consider them as paid by the masters.

Working Classes.

We now come to the Taxation of the Manual Labour Classes, who differ so widely in town and country in many portions of their expenditure. Instead of relying on any general estimate, I have obtained returns from a great number of places of the actual expenditure of fifty temperate families, and have arranged them in four groups, representing West London, East London, the Towns, and the Villages. These returns are quite distinct from those mentioned in Chapters XIII. and XIV., and are in most cases from different correspondents. Fifteen families in one large printing establishment sent their own returns direct to me under cover, embracing earnings from £50 up to £135 a year, and very various expenditures. My thanks are due to them, as well as to my other correspondents who have taken so much trouble to procure accurate information. In some places, and particularly in

Taxes on Expenditure.

Ireland, the attempt failed through the suspiciousness of the poor, and their unwillingness to disclose their own affairs. I should fear that a Wage Census, suggested last year by Dr. Farr as an addition to the general Census in 1871, would prove a failure from this cause. I am told that even the returns here given are below the actual amounts in two things; first, by the account of earnings not including extra work, and, in many cases, the children's wages; and, second, by omitting casual expenditure on Beer and Spirits. But it is believed. that the per centage on the omitted income balances the omitted expenditure. The quantity of Sugar is also below the average, from its variable consumption and from the families whose returns were procurable happening to include a majority of small consumers of that article.

The four groups of families are summarized in the following Tables from more detailed summaries which will be found in Appendix III. The West and East London families ought properly to be averaged together, since they refer to the same fraction of the nation. They are given separately, to show the difference between high and low wages in expenditure and taxation.

Taxes on Expenditure.

CHAP. XVII.

TAXATION OF METROPOLITAN WORKING MEN.

	4. West London Workmen. Average of Fifteen Families of Printers in Westminster.		5. East London Workmen. Average of Six Families of Artisans in Bethnal Green and Whitechapel.	
	Family and Income.	Taxes per Family.	Family and Income.	Taxes per Family.
Number in Family	4½		6	
	£ s. d.	£ s. d.	£ s. d.	£ s. d.
Earnings	92 0 0		53 10 0	
Rent	25 0 0		13 7 6	
I. *Rates* (paid by Landlord)	6 12 0		4 6 0	
Tenant's half rates	. . . .	3 6 0	. . . .	2 3 0
	Consumption per head. lbs.		Consumption per head. lbs.	
II. *Corn, Tea,* &c.—				
Corn		0 2 3		0 3 0
Tea	4½	0 10 6	3½	0 9 6
Coffee	4	0 5 3	1	0 1 4
Sugar	33½	0 12 6	25	0 12 2
		1 10 6		1 6 0
III. *Alcohol and Tobacco—*				
Tobacco	1½	1 1 0	1	1 1 8
	Galls.		Galls.	
Beer	23	0 17 6	6	0 5 10
Spirits	½	0 15 6	¼	0 7 6
		2 14 0		1 15 0
	Total £	7 10 6	Total £	5 4 0
Per centage of Taxes on Earning		8		9¾

The large per centage of Rates, 3½ and 4 per cent. on the Earnings, deserves attention, and should be compared with the small per centages of one and one half per cent. in the towns and villages.

In towns, even if the rates are high, the rents on which they are paid are usually low, and form a great contrast to the high rents and rates combined of London.

TAXATION OF TOWN AND COUNTRY WORKING MEN.

	6. TOWN WORKMEN. Average of Thirteen Families of Artisans and Workmen, at Abbey Town (Cumberland), Wakefield, Sheffield, and Christchurch (Hampshire).		7. AGRICULTURAL LABOURERS. Average of Thirteen Families in Yorkshire, Essex, Hampshire, and Devon.	
	Family and Income.	Taxes per Family.	Family and Income.	Taxes per Family.
	£ s. d.	£ s. d.	£ s. d.	£ s. d.
Number of Family .	5½		5½	
Earnings	57 10 0		40 0 0	
Rent	6 8 3		4 6 9	
I. *Rates—*	. 1 5 3		0 9 3	
Tenant's half rates	. . . .	0 12 6	. . . .	0 4 7
	Consumption per head. lbs.		Consumption per head. lbs.	
II. *Corn, Tea, &c.—*				
Corn . . .		0 2 9		0 2 9
Tea . . .	4	0 11 0	2¾	0 6 0
Coffee . .	4½	0 6 1		0 0 10
Sugar . .	18⅓	0 8 6	13	0 5 10
		1 8 4		0 15 5
III. *Alcohol and Tobacco—*				
Tobacco . .	1¼	1 7 7	⅘	0 14 6
	Galls.		Galls.	
Beer . . .	18½	0 17 0	6	0 5 0
Spirits . .	¾	0 10 6	—	—
		2 15 1		0 19 6
	Total £	4 15 11	Total £	1 19 6
Per centage of Taxes on Earnings .	8⅓		 5	

In all the foregoing Tables the License Duties on Brewers and Beer-sellers are included in the 2*d.* per gallon of Beer, and those on Distillers and Spirit-sellers in the 7*s.* 9*d.* per diluted gallon of British Spirits, which are charged as the Taxation on those articles.

112   *Taxes on Expenditure.*

Chap. XVII.

Thus Agricultural Labourers are both less highly rated and consume fewer taxable articles than town Workmen.

Pressure of these Taxes in England.

To show the pressure of the different Taxes on Expenditure, it is necessary to look at the following Table, constructed from the preceding summaries :—

PERCENTAGES TO INCOME OF THE TAXES ON EXPENDITURE.

	1. On Houses and Establishments.	2. On Corn, Tea, &c.	3. On Alcohol, and Tobacco.	4. Total on Expenditure.
	Per cent.	Per cent.	Per cent.	Per cent.
Upper Classes—				
1. £5,000 a year .	3·25	·25	1·	4·5
Upper Middle Classes				
2. £500 a year . .	2·7	·8	1·5	5·
Lower Middle Classes—				
3. £99 a year . .	2·5	2·	3·3	7·8
Working Classes—				
4 and 5. London (average) . .	3·8	2·	3·2	9·
6. Towns . . .	1·	2·4	5·	8·4
7. Villages . . .	·5	2·	2·5	5·

Corrections necessary.

But the averages for the Working Classes contained in the last three lines require correction for deficiency in two things—the amount of earnings and the expenditure on alcohol; and for excess in one thing—the amount of Rates.

Judging from these figures, which represent accurately the payments for rates in London, it might naturally be supposed that these Rates press very heavily upon the whole of the Working Classes, and absorb a serious per centage of their total income. But inquiry shows that their relative magnitude and pressure in proportion to earnings in the Metropolis are exceptional, and are lost in the far wider area of low rating throughout the country. Even where rates are high in other places, their pressure is much less, from the lowness of rents. Thus, in some large towns, the rates are 7s. in the pound, but the current rent of a workman's house is 2s. 6d. a week; or £6 10s. a year, rated at £5; so that he pays only £1 15s. a year rates instead of the £4 6s. at Whitechapel.

Another cause of diminution of the rating burden is the number of excusals. The average number of persons receiving parochial relief is a million, who are of course excused, and there are always a large additional number of families who are too poor to be called on for any rates.

A third cause is the prevalence in large towns of the lodging system. Mr. Gladstone's Blue-book of 1866 gave returns of the Working Classes, and the number of occupiers in all the Boroughs of England and Wales. The population was 9,300,000, so that there were about 1,300,000 Working Class families, reckoning five to each family. Yet, after making every allowance for female tenants, there were only 1,050,000 Working Class Occupiers. Their aggregate Rental was also comparatively small, amounting to less than £8,000,000 out of a total Borough Rental of £41,000,000. It would be still less in proportion in the Counties.

The following division of the £18,500,000 of Annual Rates gives a full proportion to the Working Classes :—

RATES, 1867.

(1) Land, Railways, &c., and business premises	£6,500,000
(2) Houses of the Upper and Middle Classes	8,000,000
(3) Houses of the Working Classes	4,000,000
Total	£18,500,000

Of the second and third items, one half must be counted as falling upon the Landlords, and the other half on the Tenants; so that the Rates which are ultimately borne by the Working Classes can only be estimated at £2,000,000. But this makes the injustice of their high rates in London still more glaring.

CHAPTER XVIII.

COMPARATIVE TOTAL TAXATION.

THE best way of arriving at a just idea of the Comparative Taxation of the two great sections of the community will be to add up the total taxes which can be reasonably estimated to be borne by each. This can be done by a careful comparison of the data given in the preceding pages, and it will be found worked out in detail in Appendix IV.

The first point is the Aggregate Income of each section. The calculations on this subject are stated at length in my work on National Income, but may be here given in a more simple form, using for the Upper and Middle Classes a return which has just been issued.

<small>CHAP. XVIII.
Upper and Middle and Manual Labour Classes.</small>

<small>Their Aggregate Incomes.</small>

<small>"National Income," chap. iii. p. 64, and Appendix V. p. 96.</small>

<small>The statements of the Inland Revenue Commissioners respecting the very large amount of Unreturned Profits under Schedule D—which they estimate at £57,000,000, but against which must be set a considerable amount of surcharges—leave no doubt that my calculation of the Upper and Middle Class Income is within the mark.</small>

I. Upper and Middle Classes.

<small>Chap. XVIII. 12th Inland Revenue Report, pp. 17–24.</small>

Income returned as charged to Income Tax for the year ending April 5th, 1867 . . . . . . £374,000,000

Estimate of Income excused as below £60, exempt as below £100, and Unreturned Profits . . . 116,000,000

Total £490,000,000

II. Manual Labour Class.

Income of the Manual Labour Class . . . £325,000,000

Total United Kingdom . . £815,000,000

The amount for the Manual Labour Class is considerably below the £418,000,000 estimated by <small>Professor Levi, "Working Classes."</small> Professor Leone Levi, an estimate which was made before the general lowering of wages, caused by the financial disasters of 1866, and which gives a very insufficient allowance for loss of work and old age, calculating nearly full time wages for persons of all ages up to sixty years. The estimate of £325,000,000, which makes careful allowance for both these points, is safer for purposes of Taxation.

<small>Number.</small> The second point is the number of individuals in these two sections. These were calculated from the <small>"National Income," pp. 7–16.</small> Census Tables in the same work, and may be thus given :—

United Kingdom, 1867.

	Persons.
Upper and Middle Classes . . .	6,700,000
Manual Labour Class	23,000,000
Total population . .	30,000,000

But in calculating the consumption of tea, sugar, and beer, the house servants—chiefly females—to the number of 1,300,000, must be added to the households of their Upper and Middle Class employers, and deducted from the Manual Labour Class, making the number for this purpose 8,000,000 and 22,000,000.

The third point is the amount of Taxation. The following table presents the results, leaving the long catalogue of taxes, and the reasons for their allotment to either column to be consulted in Appendix IV. Two main difficulties presented themselves: first, the division of the Taxes on Trades, Mercantile matters, and Conveyance between the two sections—in which the chief portion appears to be due to the Upper and Middle Classes, whose income is mainly spent in articles of Commerce; and second, the division of Alcoholic expenditure.

A distinction ought to be made in the latter between the expenditure of temperate families on the scale usual in their rank of life, which gives a moderate and calculable Taxation; and an immoderate or excessive expenditure, which takes place by fits and starts, is not controlled or bounded by reason, and too often is only stopped by pecuniary exhaustion. On the temperate expenditure the Customs and Excise duties are a tax, on the intemperate expenditure they are a fine and a penalty. I have endeavoured in a former chapter to distinguish between these two expenditures with the best information that I have been able to procure, and derived from no teetotal sources. Total abstainers will be likely to demur altogether to the proposition that a consumption which pays taxes to the amount of £22,000,000 on Alcohol and Tobacco, or £15,500,000 on Alcohol alone, can be a temperate and allowable consumption for thirty millions of persons. But a regular consumption of this extent —if distributed over the population—would be considerably below the consumption which is universally considered unobjectionable in the case of temperate persons in the Upper and Middle classes. It is the excessive consumption by a comparatively small number of individuals, both in steady soaking and irregular drinking bouts, that constitutes the chief portion of the intemperance of the country.

Excess in spirituous liquors cannot be said to be confined to the Working Classes. Though the Upper and Middle Classes are guilty of little drunkenness, they are too often in the habit of drinking more than is wholesome.

Comparative Taxation.

Chap. XVIII.
See Appendix IV.

	UPPER AND MIDDLE CLASSES.		MANUAL LABOUR CLASS.	
	Income.	Per centage Taxes on Income.	Income.	Per centage Taxes on Income.
INCOME	£ 490,000,000		£ 325,000,000	
TAXATION.				
I. ON INCOME:	Taxes.		Taxes.	
(1) On *Property and Income* .	13,746,000			
(2) Part on *Trades, Mercantile and Conveyance*	1,274,000			
(3) *Rates* on Land, Railways, &c., and Landlords' half on houses	12,500,000			
	27,520,000	5·6		
II. ON EXPENDITURE:				
(1) *Houses and Miscellaneous* .	11,040,000	2·2	3,426,000	1·1
(2) *Corn, Tea, Sugar, &c.* . .	4,284,000	·9	6,056,000	1·8
(3) *Alcohol and Tobacco:*				
(a) Temperate Expenditure	9,056,000	1·9	13,140,000	4·1
	24,380,000	5	22,622,000	7
Total	51,900,000	10·6	22,622,000	7
(b) Excessive or Intemperate Alcoholic Expenditure	2,100,000	·4	6,490,000	2·
GRAND TOTAL . .	£54,000,000	11	£29,112,000	9

The principal deductions from this table are as follow:—

Taxation in Proportion to Revenue and Earnings. All Classes.

1. Taken on the *Temperate Consumption* of Beer and Spirits, the Taxation of the United Kingdom appears to be thus divided:—

Upper and Middle Classes, 10½ *per cent.*
Manual Labour Class, 7 *per cent.*

Or, to put it in another way—out of an Income of £50 a temperate Workman is untaxed on £17, and pays at the same rate as the Upper and Middle Classes (10½ per cent.) on £33.

2. Including the *Intemperate and Excessive Consumption* of Beer and Spirits, the Taxation appears to be:—

Upper and Middle Classes, 11 *per cent.*
Manual Labour Class, 9 *per cent.*

But I submit that the temperate consumption is the fair scale by which to estimate.

3. The average *Taxes on Income* borne by the Upper and Middle Classes, and from which there is no honest way of escape, are 5½ per cent., and their average *Taxes on Expenditure*—which they can lessen by economy—are 5 per cent. on their revenue.

4. The Taxes of the Manual Labour Class appear to bear the following average proportion to their Earnings:—

1. *Houses and Miscellaneous,* about 1 *per cent.*

2. *Corn, Tea, Sugar, and Coffee,* nearly 2 *per cent.*

3. *Alcohol and Tobacco* (temperate consumption), 4 *per cent.*

Comparative Total Taxation.

But if the intemperate consumption is included, the last figures must stand :— Chap. XVIII.

3. *Total Alcohol and Tobacco, 6 per cent.*

Thus the main weight of the taxation of the Working Classes is on their *Alcohol and Tobacco*. It constitutes more than half the burden on the average of temperate families, and far more than half on the intemperate. Alcohol and Tobacco.

The next heaviest item is made up by the duties on *Corn, Tea, Coffee, and Sugar*, which will be seen by the table on page 112 to average 2 per cent. on all Incomes under £100 a year, nearly 1 per cent. at £500 a year, and 5s. per cent. at £5,000. Corn, Tea, &c. compared with those of Upper and Middle Classes.

The Rates and Miscellaneous Taxes are on the average of the United Kingdom the lowest of all the taxes on the Working Classes, but they press with extreme inequality, varying in the instances given in Appendix III. from 3s. on £36, or 8s. per cent. near Christchurch to 43s. on £53 10s. or £4 per cent in Whitechapel; a state of things which urgently calls for reformation. Rates, &c.

If any one should think that the above calculations are below the actual Taxation borne by the Working Classes, and that they are taxed as heavily as the Upper and Middle Classes, he should consult the Summary of Taxation given by Professor Leone Levi, at page 43 of the Introduction to the "Wages and Earnings of the Working Classes," published in 1867.

Professor Levi says :—

" Our workmen have no reason to complain of the extent of Taxation

CHAP. XVIII.

pressing upon them. There was a time when corn was taxed 25s. a quarter, tea 100 per cent., sugar as much as 2d. to 3d. a pound, and when bacon, butter, cheese, soap, and candles were all taxed, raising the prices of food probably by at least a third of the amount in tax and monopoly. Now the taxes are greatly diminished, and they are so levied that a working man, of sober and abstemious habits, may be said to bear but a very small share indeed of the national burdens."

Professor Levi then estimates the Taxation of the *Working Classes* as £24,000,000, and their income as £418,000,000; which gives a percentage of Taxes to Income of 5¼ *per cent.*

He estimates the Taxation of the *Upper and Middle Classes* as £50,000,000, and their Income as a little below that of the Working Classes; so that we may take it at £400,000,000, giving a percentage of Taxation of 12½ *per cent.*

Edinburgh Review.

A previous estimate was made by an eminent writer in the *Edinburgh Review*, of January 1860.

Working Classes: . . . Income, £225,000,000.
Taxes, £24,500,000.
Or 11 per cent.

Upper and Middle Classes: Income, £320,500,000.
Taxes, £51,500,000.
Or 16 per cent.

Thus both these Estimates, which include the total Alcoholic expenditure, make the Taxation of the Working Classes much less in proportion to the Upper and Middle Classes than my Estimate.

CHAPTER XIX.

LAND, PERSONALTY, AND INDUSTRY.

Such is a general view of the Comparative Taxation of the two great sections of the community. But what inequalities underlie this average distribution of the burden? *[margin: Chap. XIX. Inequalities of Taxation.]*

In the Upper and Middle Classes there are three great divisions of Income, which bear, as we have seen, in their character of Income, very different amounts of Taxation. *[margin: Taxes on Income, see pp. 97 and 99.]*

Real Property Incomes taxed at 11 per cent.
Personalty Incomes taxed at 7 per cent.
Industrial Incomes taxed at $3\frac{1}{2}$ per cent.

The average of the three has just been shown to be nearer the last, being $5\frac{1}{2}$ per cent. To obtain their *total Taxation*, we must add to these per centages, which are for the Taxes on Income only, the percentages of the Taxes on Expenditure. Suppose three persons with incomes of £5,000 a year, the *[margin: Add Taxes on Expenditure.]*

124   *Land, Personalty, and Industry.*

CHAP. XIX.

Incomes of £5,000, see Table p. 107.

first income derived solely from Real Property, the second from Personalty, and the third Industrial; the first two keeping up the same kind of establishment, and paying for it an equal amount of taxes, which may be estimated at £220; but the possessor of the Industrial Income, who has to provide for Insurance or Savings, keeping up an establishment less by one-fourth, and paying one-fifth less Taxes on Expenditure.

TAXES ON £5,000 A YEAR.

Taxes.	From Realty.	From Personalty.	Industrial.
On Income	£ 550	£ 350	£ 175
On Expenditure . . .	220	220	175
Total	£770	£570	£350
Per centage on Income .	15½	11½	7

In these examples the Income from Personalty pays £200 less Taxes than Income of the same amount from Real Property; and the Industrial Income (even if conscientiously returned to Income Tax) pays £220 less than the Income from Personalty; and £420 less than the Income from Realty. These are large differences of Taxation, and greater than those which were thought equitable at page 98. ^{CHAP. XIX.}

Take, in a similar manner, three Incomes at £500 a year, the first two with establishments on an equal scale, which may pay taxes to the amount of £26 a year, and the Industrial Income a smaller establishment paying one-seventh less taxes on Expenditure. ^{Incomes of £500, see Table p. 107.}

TAXES ON £500 A YEAR.

Taxes.	From Realty.	From Personalty.	Industrial.
On Income	£ 55	£ 35	£　s. 17　10
On Expenditure . . .	26	26	22　10
Total	£81	£61	£40
Per centage on Income .	16	12	8.

Thus the Trader with £500 a year pays £21 less taxes than an interest in personalty of the same annual amount, and £41 less taxes than a similar income derived from Land. These are large differences for such a scale of income.

Take again Incomes at £99 a year, below Income Tax, and also below any appreciable expenditure in stamps; but each paying on his household expenditure taxes of £8 a year. The taxes will be ^{Incomes of £99. See p. 107.}

TAXES ON £99 A YEAR.

Taxes.	From Realty.	From Personalty.	Industrial.
	£ s.	£ s.	£
On Income	8 10	4 10	—
On Expenditure . . .	8 0	8 0	8
Total and per centages .	£16 10	£12 10	£8

These again are very considerable differences on such small incomes.

General Comparison. But the per centages in these three tables enable us to make another generalization, and to show how the average Upper and Middle Class Taxation of 10½ per cent., when split up into its three kinds of income, contrasts with the Taxation on the Industrial Incomes of the Working Classes.

UPPER AND MIDDLE CLASS TAXATION on
    Landed Incomes . . . . . 16 *per cent.*
    Personalty Incomes . . . . 12 *per cent.*
    Industrial Incomes, not quite 8 *per cent.*

WORKING CLASS TAXATION on
    Industrial Earnings,
      (temperate expenditure) . . 7 *per cent.*

Thus compared with the scale on page 98 the Land has to pay 1½ per cent. on its Income too much in Taxes, while Industry pays on its Income 1 per cent. too little. Nor, as compared with the Working Classes, does it seem fair that the possessor of £5,000 or even £500 a year from an Industrial Income with so many more comforts and luxuries and means of saving, should pay so nearly the same Taxation as the temperate working man, who can afford no luxuries and can scarcely lay by any savings. This anomaly will appear still more striking, when we come to the next head of the inquiry.

CHAPTER XX.

THE EXTRA COST OF TAXES.

<small>Chap. XX.</small>

WHAT is the real cost of the Taxes? Do they take out of the pockets of the Tax-payers more or less than the amounts which they produce, or ought to produce, to the Treasury?

In pursuing this inquiry it is necessary to remember that no Tax can be perfect. Mr. McCulloch very justly remarks, that it may be said of Taxes as of poems,

> "Whoe'er expects a faultless tax to see,
> Expects what neither is, nor was, nor e'er shall be."

<small>Cost of Collection.</small>

The first point to be ascertained is the cost of Collection—a necessary item in every Tax. For the Local Taxes there are no means of ascertaining this amount. For the Imperial Taxes it may be collected from the public accounts, remembering that the Coast Guard is kept up as a Reserve for the Navy, and is under the control of the Admiralty, and that, apart from this object, a Special Preventive Service at one-third of the cost would fulfil the duties with equal efficiency. But allotting half the cost, the summary is as follows:—

COST OF COLLECTION.

CUSTOMS.	£	£
Salaries, Expenses, and Superannuations	944,000	
Half the Expense of the Coast Guard and Pensions	386,000	
		1,330,000
INLAND REVENUE.		
Salaries, Expenses, and Superannuations		1,510,000
Total		£2,840,000

This is a cost of 6 per cent. on the £22,650,000 of Customs Duties, and of nearly 4 per cent. on the £39,400,000 of Inland Revenue. But both are really portions of one system, and their cost must be reckoned together. So long as there are Duties on British Spirits, there must be Duties on Foreign Spirits, and the Custom House Establishment must be kept up at nearly the same expense. Both Excise and Customs are necessary parts of the machinery for the Taxation of Alcoholic Liquors, a Taxation which can scarcely be dispensed with either on financial or moral grounds. Hence the larger cost of collection of Customs Duties is no argument against their retention, and imposes no hardship on one class of the community more than on another.

CHAP. XX.
Unequal Collection.

The second point of inquiry is this: Does the mode of collection exact more than is due from any one class of Tax-payers, and obtain less than is due from another?

This is the case with the Income Tax. Land and Houses are assessed on rack-rent, with no allowance for repairs, insurance, cost of management, or abatements of rent, items which Mr. Gladstone considered legitimate deductions in order to ascertain net income, and which he estimated at 16 per cent. So that a Tax of 5*d.* in the pound, or 2 per cent. on the gross income, is a Tax of £2 out of £84, or $2\frac{1}{3}$ per cent. upon net income; being an overcharge of *one-third* per cent.

Budget Speech, 1853, p. 24.

On the other hand, Industrial Incomes under Schedule D are self-assessed, and, according to the calculations of the Inland Revenue Commissioners, understate their profits on the average by £57 out of £158, or 36 per cent. But this calculation must be taken with considerable allowance. It is based upon London returns, where the increase of profits and the opportunities of concealment are greatest. It cannot be accepted as a rule for the country, where profits are more stationary and every man's income well known. Against it must be set off the numerous cases of declining businesses, where too large an assessment is paid to keep up appear-

Twelfth Inland Revenue Report.

The Extra Cost of Taxes.

ances, and the still more numerous instances where surcharges are submitted to from indisposition to undergo the annoyance and loss of time of an appeal. The net balance of unreturned profits over the whole country, after deducting surcharges, is more probably 25 per cent. But this reduces a 5*d.* Income Tax from 2 to 1½ per cent.; being an undercharge of *one-half* per cent. Chap. XX.

The third question is of a more complicated nature: Do any Taxes, by their indirect effects, cost the Taxpayer more than what he pays to the Tax Collector? Additional cost to the Taxpayer.

Among Taxes on Income, the *Land Tax* is an example. It produces £1,093,000. But the Landowners have redeemed a yearly amount of £944,000, so that the tax actually costs them, in present payments and capital sunk, or extra price of land, a total per annum of £2,037,000, or *three-fourths* per cent. on their income beyond what they now pay to the State. Land Tax.

Another example is *Probate Duty*, which costs the owner of Personalty 2⅔ per cent. instead of the 2 per cent. which he has paid to the State, being an extra cost of *two-thirds* per cent. on the Income of the property. Probate Duty, see p. 28.

Similarly, the *Legacy Duty* really costs the legatees of personal property, and of real property Legacy Duty, see p. 20.

devised for sale, 3⅓ per cent., instead of the 2½ per cent. which is actually received by the State; being an extra cost to them of nearly 1 per cent. on the same Income.

Customs and Excise Duties.

But the Customs and Excise Duties are commonly considered to be the chief offenders, by raising the prices of the Articles which they tax beyond the amount of duty exacted.

p. 68.

Corn is a clear instance, where the shilling per quarter duty on imports appears to raise the price of all the corn in the kingdom by an equal amount, and costs the families of the poor about $9d.$ per head for wheat, barley, and other grain, beyond the $6d.$ per head which they pay in the tax itself.

With respect to the other articles subject to Customs Duties, there has been much controversy.

Custom House formalities.

The Custom House formalities and delays have been accused of occasioning an additional cost to the public of millions sterling; and Tea was especially cited as an instance where the price is largely increased on this account. But on inquiry of the leading mercantile houses, I find these statements condemned as entirely groundless and fallacious. I have before me the report of a very experienced Tea Inspector of one of the largest importing houses,—endorsed by his prin-

Tea.

cipals,—calculating the total Custom House ex- CHAP. XX.
penses incurred by all the firms engaged in that
Trade as £12,000; a mere nothing compared
with the value of the Imports, or the £2,300,000
paid as duty.

The same house adds,

"In reference to Tea, we are persuaded that it is the easiest collected Customs Duty we have, and that it involves very moderate cost to the public in any form."

Sugar has also been given as an instance of great Sugar.
loss to the public from the effect of Duties. But
the loss is stated to arise from the working of the
differential duties, a controversy in which there are
the most various opinions, and where the judgment
of Mr. Gladstone was in their favour. The firms
with whom I communicated stated the universal
feeling of the trade to be that the differential duties
are a mistake, but said that the average loss of
sugar which they caused was considerably under
ten per cent. This, however, is an objection to a
particular form of Duty, and not to the Duty
itself.

But the great objection to Customs and Excise Interest on Duties.
Duties is that they are paid by the trader, who
charges interest upon them to the public; so that
the Duty is ultimately paid by the public in an
aggravated form. The amount of increase has been

CHAP. XX.

variously stated as from one to fifty per cent., and the total calculated at correspondingly small or large sums. But the best way of obtaining a clear idea on the subject will be to ascertain the total value of the commodities taxed, and the proportions in which it is divided between the Producer and Shipper, the Government, and the Wholesale and Retail Dealers. The two first amounts can, in most cases, be deduced from the official returns of the Statistical Abstract. The last must be obtained from the Trade. This has been done in the Tables in Appendix V., to which I must refer for details and explanations, only premising that the prices quoted are those of respectable shops, and do not include the excessive profits of the petty retail trade.

Tea, Coffee, and Sugar.

I.—VALUE OF TEA, COFFEE, AND SUGAR CONSUMED IN 1867.

	£
Tea	14,800,000
Coffee and Chicory	2,318,000
Sugar, sold to private consumers	21,600,000
Total private consumption	£38,718,000

This is exclusive of the Sugar used by Brewers, Confectioners, &c. The average prices on which it is based are: *Tea*, 2s. 8d. per lb., *Coffee and Chicory*, 1s. 5d. per lb., *Sugar*, 4½d. per lb.

Appendix V. Table 1.

This total is divisible into four parts, the first and second of which are taken (except as regards Chicory) from the Statistical Abstract.

II.—DUTY, PROFIT, AND VALUE OF TEA, COFFEE, AND SUGAR CONSUMED IN 1867.

	£	Per centage on Total Value.
1. Value before paying Duty, or "short price"	21,878,000	56
2. Duty	8,087,000	21
3. Refining or Roasting	2,570,000	7
4. Wholesale and Retail Traders' Profit, Expenses, and Interest on Capital	6,183,000	16
Total Value	£38,718,000	100

The small amount of the Profit is owing to the custom of the retail dealers of selling Sugar at a very small profit, or without any profit at all. The Profits estimated are, *Tea* 7*d.* per lb., *Coffee and Chicory*, 4*d.* per lb., *Sugar*, ½*d.* per lb.; being 22 per cent., 24 per cent., and 11 per cent.

A book of some authority on prices of food, Dodd's "Food of London," published in 1856, gives the average profit of brokers and dealers in tea as having been 8*d.* per lb. when the duty was 2*s.* 2*d.*; so that the profit seems to have slightly diminished during the thirteen years.

In answer to many inquiries, I gather from the Trade that interest is undoubtedly charged by the retail dealer on his advances for Duty, but that it is impossible to ascertain the rate, since he does not compute it per lb. or per cent., but simply mixes his tea or coffee so as to obtain the usual profit per lb. But that if the duty on tea or coffee were

CHAP. XX.

removed the public would ultimately receive the reduction of duty, and about ten per cent. in addition, if the prices did not rise in China, a contingency which would be exceedingly probable, and which has already taken place on previous reductions of duty. So that practically ten per cent. may be said to be the amount of interest paid by the public on the Tea and Coffee Duties.

The circumstances of Sugar are different. The reduction of the Sugar Duties would give to the Trade an opportunity of obtaining some profit from the article, and the public would gain only part of the reduction and no interest.

Alcohol.

Alcoholic Liquors are much greater in value.

Appendix V.
Table 2.

III.—VALUE OF WINE, BEER, AND SPIRITS CONSUMED IN 1867.

	£
Wine	10,200,000
Beer	42,500,000
Spirits, British	21,600,000
Ditto Foreign and Colonial	9,730,000
Total	£84,030,000

The prices per gallon in this estimate are: Wine, 15s., Beer, 1s., British Spirits, 15s., Foreign and Colonial Spirits, 20s. 6d., and do not include the excessive retail prices per glass, quart, or quartern, which are charged in public-houses.

The division of this total is as follows :—

The Extra Cost of Taxes.

IV.—Duty, Profit, and Value of Wine, Beer, and Spirits consumed in 1867.

	£	Per cent.
Value before paying Duty	31,930,000	38
Duty and Licenses	24,230,000	28½
Storage, Bottling, and Waste	2,070,000	2½
Sellers' Profits, Expenses, and Interest on Capital	26,080,000	31
Total	£84,030,000	100

The Duty averages rather more than 15 per cent. on Wine and Beer, and 46 per cent. on Spirits. The Profit is much the same in all.

Here the Interest charged upon Duty by the Trader is much larger, and is probably at the same rate as the profit itself, or 31 per cent. This amount is paid by all classes, but presses with the greatest weight upon the Working Classes, to whose Alcoholic Taxation it adds one-third, or nearly 1 per cent. on their earnings.

The Taxes on Beer and British Spirits are levied on the raw material in the process of manufacture, and the interest charged on them increases at every stage of their progress to the Consumer. This is not the case with Tea or Sugar, where the duty is paid at the last moment before consumption, either by the retailer or his immediate agent or wholesale merchant. The mode of increase in the case of Beer is shown in the following evidence of Mr. Joshua Fielden, of Todmorden (now M.P. for the East-West Riding) before the Malt Tax Committee, 1868. The principle was endorsed as correct by the Committee in their Report, with an expression of their opinion "that the consumer of Beer pays a very much heavier Tax than goes into the Exchequer." *Beer. Malt Tax Report, p. 5.*

"Question 4234. Is it your opinion that the Tax increases in pressure at every stage of manufacture? It must be so. I have here

CHAP. XX.

Malt Tax Evidence, p. 145.

a pamphlet I wrote, showing in simple figures how the Tax must increase, and I had Mr. Gladstone's support on this view (I do not say as to the actual figures) when I went on a deputation to him. He admitted that a Tax laid upon the raw commodity must increase in pressure at every stage through which it passed, and every hand through which it passed. I wrote that pamphlet to show the principle, though it may not be accurate in detail. I say that the amount of the Tax is 21s. 8d. per quarter of malt. I take the maltster's charge for interest upon the Tax which he pays at 5 per cent., and his profit at 10 per cent. ; that makes an addition of 15 per cent. to the Tax, or 3s. 3d. ; and that makes the duty charged by the maltster to the brewer 24s. 11d. The brewer's charge on that which he pays to the maltster I put down at 15 per cent., that is, 3s. 9d. ; the Tax charged by the public brewer to the retailer will be 28s. 8d. ; the retailer's charge upon the Tax I put at 10 per cent., that is, 2s. 10d. ; making the Tax charged to the consumer by the retailer 31s. 6d. ; while the amount that goes into the Exchequer is only 21s. 8d. The rate of interest and profit are what I consider, as a man of business, a fair return for a man to have upon his investment."

Mr. Fielden therefore calculates the increase of price at 45 per cent., and, making allowance for the fervour of his opposition to the Malt Tax, we may safely take it at 33 per cent.

Tobacco.

Tobacco is a very difficult subject, from the small value of the article itself before paying duty, and the great varieties of price. The lowest priced Tobacco is "Shag," which usually sells at 3d. per ounce or 4s. per pound, and is the kind used by the poorer consumers. As the lowest duty is 3s. 2d. per lb., this seems only to leave 10d. per lb. for price and profit. But water is almost as important an ingredient in low-priced Tobacco as in Spirits, and the process of "damping" adds considerably

The Extra Cost of Taxes. 139

to the weight and profit. The interest charged on the Duty may probably be taken at 15 per cent. Chap. XX.

It must be borne in mind, as to Tables II. and IV., that the amount estimated for Profit includes the Trade expenses of the merchant's counting-house and the retail dealer's shop—a very serious deduction in all cases—and also the Interest on Capital, which in the higher Wine and Spirit Trade, where those articles are kept for many years, is a very large item. When these deductions are made, it will be seen that the net profit realized is much diminished, and that there is not scope for the large increase of price in consequence of duties which is estimated by many financial writers.

A remark is also requisite respecting the habit of Working men, of buying everything in the smallest possible quantities. Driblet purchaser.

Tea is constantly bought in quarter ounces, at three farthings per packet, requiring from the shopkeeper 64 wrappings and weighings for a single pound. The price amounts to 4s. per lb. for tea which would probably be sold at 2s. 8d. per lb. in the same shop, being an increase of 50 per cent.

Tobacco is very commonly sold in "Screws" or quarter ounces at 1d., raising the price of 4s. tobacco to 5s. 4d., or 33 per cent.

Porter is sold by the publicans to go out of the house at 1s. per gallon, or 3d. per quart. But the workman prefers to take his glass "in the house" at 2d., which is 4d. per quart, an increase of 33 per cent.

CHAP. XX.

These extreme prices are often confused with the results of Taxation, but they ought to be carefully distinguished. They occur equally on untaxed articles, such as coals, butter, &c., and arise from the habits and weaknesses of consumers, and not from Taxation. The habit of purchasing with forethought would add very largely to the pecuniary means of the Working Classes.

Summary of results.

The following table will give an approximate idea of the extra cost of Taxes to the different classes of the community, as explained in the foregoing pages. Incomes below £100 may be considered as under the same circumstances with the Working Classes. The Extra Cost of the Taxes on Articles of Consumption to the Upper and Middle Classes may be averaged at *one-half* per cent. upon Income, near and above £500 a year. The table expresses the per centages in *shillings per* £100, as well as in fractions, for the sake of clearness.

It will be seen that the extra cost of Taxes is much the same in proportion among all classes, except the higher Industrial Incomes, which escape the heavy Tax on articles of Consumption that it imposes on small Incomes, and also escape the surcharges which attach to Realty and Personalty.

Extra Cost of Taxes.

	Per centage on Income.	£ s. d.
LAND AND HOUSES—		
Income Tax, overcharge	⅓	0 6 0
Capital sunk in Land Tax	¾	0 15 0
Articles of consumption	½	0 10 0
Total per cent.	1½	£1 11 0
PERSONALTY—		
Probate Duty	⅔	0 13 4
Legacy Duty	⅚	0 16 8
Articles of Consumption	½	0 10 0
Total per cent.	2	£2 0 0
WORKING CLASSES (and Incomes under £100)—		
Corn	¼	0 5 0
Alcohol	1	1 0 0
Tobacco, Tea, and Coffee	¼	0 5 0
Total per cent.	1½	£1 10 0
INDUSTRIAL INCOMES (above £400)—		
Articles of consumption	½	0 10 0
Deduct, Income Tax, undercharge	½	0 10 0
Total per cent.	0	0 0 0

CHAPTER XXI.

SUMMARY AND CONCLUSION.

<small>Chap. XXI.</small>

Every inquiry into Taxation must end with two questions. First, Do any classes of the nation pay more than their proper share—or less than their proper share—of the Taxes of the Country? Second, If there are such inequalities, how can they be remedied? Before attempting to answer, let me sum up as briefly as possible the results of this long and necessarily complicated investigation.

<small>What inequalities, and Remedies.</small>

<small>Results of Inquiry. Upper and Middle and Working Classes.</small>

A general view of the Taxation of the United Kingdom as between the two great divisions of its population, the Upper and Middle Classes, and the Manual Labour Class, was given at page 119, with the following conclusion:

1.—Comparative Taxation.

The Upper and Middle Classes have
    An Income of £490,000,000
    A Taxation of 52,000,000
   Being a per centage of 10½ per cent.

Summary and Conclusion.

The MANUAL LABOUR CLASS have
   An Income of £325,000,000
   A Taxation of 22,600,000
      Being a per centage of 7 per cent.

CHAP. XXI.

This includes only the temperate expenditure in alcoholic drinks. It reckons the tea, sugar, and beer of household servants as paid for by the Upper and Middle Classes. But it also reckons the taxation of one million of paupers, who are wholly or partially maintained by Taxes as paid by the Manual Labour Class. It is based on a careful estimate of Income, which many representatives of the Working Classes consider too low a calculation of their earnings.

On this basis the Working Classes pay *one-third less* Taxes in proportion to their incomes than the Upper and Middle Classes.

If the intemperate expenditure is added, the comparison stands thus, still making the Working Class proportion of Taxes lower by *one-fifth* :—

   2.—TAXATION, INCLUDING INTEMPERANCE.   Page 120.
    UPPER AND MIDDLE CLASSES . . 11 per cent.
    MANUAL LABOUR CLASS . . . 9 per cent.

But Intemperate Expenditure is too irregular to be called Taxation. And drunkards, in a large proportion of instances, leave their families to be supported more or less by the Poor Rate or by charity.

But, looking more narrowly into the Taxation of the Upper and Middle Classes, we found it derived from three great Classes of Income, Land, Personalty, and Industry, each paying, and justly paying, a different amount of Taxation. Taking Personalty as the standard, it appeared equitable that Landed

Land, Personalty, and Industry. See pp. 96-99, Chap. XV.

144 *Summary and Conclusion.*

CHAP. XXI.

Incomes should pay a per centage of Taxes *one-fifth* higher, and Industrial Incomes a per centage *one-fourth* lower, than Incomes from Personalty. Hence, if the Taxes on Personalty averaged 12 per cent. the scale of Taxation should be approximately as follows :

3.—NORMAL SCALE OF TAXATION.

UPPER AND MIDDLE CLASSES—
    Landed Incomes . . . . 14½ per cent.
    Personalty Incomes . . . 12 ,,
    Industrial Incomes . . . 9 ,,

MANUAL LABOUR CLASS—
    Workmen's Earnings   6 or 7 ,,

Total actual Taxation.

The actual Taxation showed much larger differences. Adding the Taxes on Incomes to those on Expenditure in examples taken from average styles of living, we found the totals to be approximately as follows :—

4.—DISTRIBUTION OF TAXATION.

See pp. 124-126, Chap. XIX.

	Taxes on Landed Incomes.	Taxes on Personalty Incomes.	Taxes on Industrial Incomes.
UPPER AND MIDDLE CLASSES —	£	£	£ s.
£5,000 a year	770	570	350 0
£500 a year	80	60	40 0
£99 a year	16	13	8 0
MANUAL LABOUR CLASS—			
£50 a year	—	—	3 10

Summary and Conclusion. 145

These instances did not include the double taxation on some kinds of property, as Leaseholds, which are taxed both as Realty and Personalty; or the Legacy Duty paid by the large portion of Real Property devised on trusts for sale.

Here the actual amounts of Taxation on Landed Incomes are much higher, and on Industrial Incomes lower, than the per centages in the normal scale.

5.—Actual per Centages of Taxation.

Upper and Middle Classes—
    Landed Incomes . . . . 16 per cent.
    Personalty Incomes . . . 12 ,,
    Industrial Incomes . . . . 8 ,,

Manual Labour Class—
    Workmen's Earnings   7

So that Land pays 1½ per cent. more, and Industrial Incomes 1 per cent. less than the fair proportion; per centages which in actual practice make a very serious difference (as shown in Table 4) in the amounts exacted. Thus an Income of £5,000 a-year from Land pays £75 a-year more than its share, and one from Industry £50 less than its share, making a total difference against the Land of 2½ per cent. or £125 a-year.

But we had still to take into account the extra cost of Taxes to Taxpayers beyond the amount actually paid into the Exchequer. This appeared to be a charge of from 1½ to 2 per cent. on all

146   *Summary and Conclusion.*

CHAP. XXI.

Incomes except the Industrial Incomes of the Middle Classes. Adding these charges to the per centages in the last Table, we have the following summary :—

G.—TOTAL COST OF TAXATION.

UPPER AND MIDDLE CLASSES—
 Landed Incomes . . . 17½ per cent.
 Personalty Incomes . . 14 ,,
 Industrial Incomes . . 8 ,,

MANUAL LABOUR CLASS—
 Workmen's Earnings   8½ ,,

The total burden of the Taxes and their extra cost, which is here divided, probably averages 11½ per cent. on the total Income of the nation.

See Chap. XVI.

Besides these classes of Income, we found some instances of Taxation, particularly in the duties on Locomotion, which showed for higher per centages; and some impolitic taxes, such as those on Insurances and Corn, which were indefensible.

See pp. 31 and 68.

First question, Inequalities.

The question, therefore, whether any classes pay more than their proper share, and whether any pay less than their proper share, of the Taxation of the country, must be thus answered.

1. There are still some flagrant imposts, like those on Locomotion, bearing hardly on small classes of persons; and some impolitic taxes, like those on

Insurance and Corn, discouraging habits of prudence, or affecting the price of articles to an extent far exceeding the amount paid into the Exchequer, that ought to be, as soon as possible, repealed.

2. The Taxation of the Manual Labour Classes—though small in proportion to that on Real Property and Personalty—appears to be heavy in proportion to the Taxation of the larger Industrial Incomes of the Upper and Middle Classes, and ought to be in some measure lightened.

3. The Taxation on Real Property—even after making allowance for the extent to which it ought to be higher than that on other kinds of Income—is too high, and out of proportion to the Taxation on the Personalty and Industrial Incomes of the Upper and Middle Classes.

4. The Taxes on Occupiers are unequal and anomalous; and, in important portions of the kingdom, oppressive.

How are these inequalities to be remedied? *Second question, Remedies.*

It is much easier to point out an injustice than to suggest a good remedy; and it is also far easier to suggest a reasonable remedy on paper than for a Minister to carry out a remedy in practice.

148   *Summary and Conclusion.*

CHAP. XXI.
Impolitic Taxes.

1. The following Taxes ought to be repealed :

Post-horses and Public Carriages	284,000
Railways	486,000
Fire Insurance	974,000
Corn	876,000
	£2,620,000

But the amount is a serious obstacle to their early abrogation, and in all probability it can only be done by degrees, as financial opportunities may offer.

Manual Labour Class Taxation. See also pp. 112 and 119.

2. The Taxation of the Manual Labour Class was shown at page 120 to be comprised in three principal heads, bearing the following proportion to their earnings :—

Houses and Miscellaneous	1 per cent.
Corn, Tea, Sugar, and Coffee	2 ,,
Alcohol and Tobacco—	
Temperate Consumption	4 ,,
Intemperate Consumption	2 ,,

Alcohol.

How can this Taxation be reduced? Taking the largest item first, the payments for Alcohol and Tobacco, there are two methods of reduction.

First, the taxes themselves might be reduced, and the trade thrown open. But it is very much to be feared that such a measure would be no boon to the Working Classes. The amount remitted by the State, and much more besides, would too probably be squandered upon increased consumption, and encourage intemperance. Cheap spirits and unlimited beerhouses have always been found to multiply drunkenness. A correspondent of the *Nonconformist* states the result as regards beer-houses :—

<small>Rev. F. White, March 17, 1869.</small>

"The experiment was tried in Liverpool. The magistrates there, a few years ago, licensed every one who applied for liberty to sell drink, so as practically to leave the trade open. The result was that two years since they were compelled to fall back upon restriction, so awful was the outbreak of intemperance in that port. The same result would certainly follow everywhere."

But it may be quite possible, by a wise alteration of the method of levying the malt-tax, to diminish the number of persons who have to pay interest on the tax before it reaches the consumer; and to encourage home brewing, with its attendant advantages of wholesomeness, economy, and freedom from public-house habits.

Second, the Taxes might be reduced by prudent restrictions on the sale of drink, and particularly by a revision of the licensing system. Take away excessive temptation, and you will greatly reduce excessive drinking. No one could lament a deficit in the Taxes on Alcohol caused by such a measure. On the contrary, it would be most desirable in the true interest of the nation.

But thirdly, in any case, stringent measures ought

CHAP. XXI.

to be taken to guard against adulteration, and mixing pernicious ingredients in beer and spirits. The labouring man, who pays such a heavy taxation on these articles, has a right to precautions for their purity. Every monopoly ought to be put under strict regulation by the State, and malpractices to be sharply looked after and punished.

Corn, Tea, Coffee, and Sugar.

Let us turn next to the Taxes on Tea, Coffee, Sugar, and Corn, amounting to 2 per cent. on earnings. These will be reduced by the repeal of the Corn Duty. Their effect may also be lightened by the repeal of the licenses for selling Tea and Coffee, which constitute a serious tax on small shopkeepers, and lessen the competition which is so necessary for low prices.

But the objection to the repeal of the Tea, Coffee, and Sugar Duties is this. Is it wise to rest the Taxation of any large class of the community almost entirely on Alcohol and Tobacco?—Taxes, the former of which, however necessary, still partake of the character of blood money. It would be tempting the State,—almost obliging the State,—to foster and wink at the liquor traffic, for the sake of its contribution to her revenue.

There is an argument in favour of their repeal, that it would give an important impetus to Trade. Let us see what it amounts to. It is shown in

Summary and Conclusion.

Table 1 of Appendix V. that the total value before paying Duty of the Tea imported is under £9,000,000, of the Coffee about £1,000,000, and of the Sugar (allowing for public consumption) about £13,000,000. Suppose for the sake of argument that these quantities were increased 33 per cent. by the repeal of the Duties, the increase of Imports would be £7,500,000. Suppose them increased by 50 per cent. it would be £11,500,000. Both sums are small compared with our total Imports of £275,000,000, and, even if realized, could scarcely be said to exercise upon Trade an influence of magnitude.

2, 3, & 4. The Local Rates are the last subject of inquiry. How are we to remedy their oppressiveness on the London poor, the excess of taxation which they occasion on Real Property, and the inconveniences they inflict upon all occupiers?

Theoretically they offend against the elementary laws of political economy. They are guilty of great inequality, differing in every one of the Unions and Union-parishes of the United Kingdom, and varying from 6d. in the £1 in some favoured parishes up to 9s. in the £1 in Bethnal Green, and even higher in more distressed localities. They are uncertain in the times and amount of collection. They are levied in a manner which is inconvenient to the poorer ratepayers. But they have the great practical merit of keeping down expenditure, and of saving millions which would be spent under a more pleasant mode of taxation.

Local Equalization.

(1) Their inequality as between neighbouring Unions is one of their most striking hardships, and it is aggravated by the fact that the parishes of the poor in large cities are, by the local character of the tax, much more heavily rated than the parishes of the rich. A partial remedy is obvious,—to extend the Unions so as in every case to include the wealthier quarters with those of the poorer inhabitants. Belgravia and the City ought to contribute to the destitution of Whitechapel and Shoreditch. It is in the highest degree unjust that cities of the poor at one end of London should be ground down by twice or three times the poundage of Rates paid by cities of the rich at the other end of London. Difficulty of management or even of economy is no excuse for injustice. In order to relieve the excessive taxation of the dwellings of the Metropolitan poor, equalization of Metropolitan Rates is absolutely necessary. Controlling committees must be organized to keep down wastefulness. The same applies in other great towns.

(2) But both the poor and the landowners have another cause of complaint, in the small area of income which is liable to these taxes. A hundred

Summary and Conclusion. 153

and forty millions of Rental bear eighteen and a half millions of Local Taxes; an amount which has been constantly increased, and is continually increasing. If the burden were stationary, it might be of less consequence. But the progress of improvement ensures its growing larger. The landowners are fully justified in pointing to their excess of Taxation, which is entirely owing to it, and to the fact that this excess is constantly augmenting; and in asking that Personal Property and Industrial Incomes, whose total Taxation, as we have seen, is too low in proportion to that of Land, should bear some portion of the burden. The poor in the heavily-rated cities would derive benefit from bringing into contribution these accumulations of income. A small Rate in aid, say of $1\frac{1}{2}d.$ in the £1, upon Schedules D and E, ought to be added to the Poor Rate. The mode of its allotment, whether according to the locality of the taxpayer, or by application to a distinct branch of Poor Rate expenditure—such as that on Lunatics—need cause no serious difficulty.

Chap. XXI.
Extension of area of Incomes rated.

(3) But a third hardship remains. Rates on Occupiers, as we have seen, are a composite Tax, which is really paid part by the Owner and part by the Occupier. To exact it all from the Workman, distress-warrant in hand, is to make him

Separation of Owners' and Occupier Rates.
See Chap. XII.

believe himself more heavily taxed than he really is. It tends to make him discontented with the State. It inflicts a real hardship, because it levies his landlord's rent at inconvenient times and instalments, and probably costs him more in pawnbroker's interest or temporary deprivation of food. Cannot we find some means of separating his own portion of the Tax from that of his landlord, and leave each to pay his real liability?

Another reason for such a course exists in the Parliamentary franchise. When that franchise was given, every one believed that the Occupier who paid his rates was the real and ultimate payer. Most people went to a further extreme, and maintained that when the landlord paid the rates the tenant was the real and ultimate payer. The inference was obvious. Let the tenant actually pay what he really pays, and renew the old law of England, by which the ratepayers were the voters. There are two great advantages in such a system, that the actual ratepayer is more accurately registered, and more worthy of the franchise. On the other hand, the compounded tenant, whose rates are paid for him, is apt to be inaccurately registered, and less worthy of the franchise.

To restore compounding as regards the whole rate paid by the Occupier will be to adopt the

Summary and Conclusion. 155

latter disadvantages. A lower class of voters—called by Mr. Bright the "residuum"—will be brought in; and the rate-book will be rendered unreliable—nay, positively misleading—as an Occupation Register; since it is not in human nature that Overseers should be constantly correcting long lists of Occupiers with whom they have nothing to do.

I suggest that the Landlords' and Tenants' portion of the Local Rates on each tenement held for less than a term of three months should be separated by the larger portion of the Rate being thrown upon the Landlords; and a small invariable tax, say 1s. 6d. per quarter (6s. per annum), be levied on every family or adult male occupying a distinct room or tenement with less than £100 income,—with power of excusal by the magistrates. The latter tax, the one on the occupier, should be collected with the Income Tax, and applied to the Poor Rate; and the Income Tax books, instead of the Poor Rate books, should be made the basis for the Register; four quarters' payment entitling to the vote. In this way we should secure three advantages: a reliable Register, more responsible and careful Voters, and a direct Tax, which if successful might be used to reduce the Taxes on articles of consumption.

It may be objected that the Tenant would still really pay part of the Rate imposed on the Landlords. But I think not, and for this reason. A tax tends to fix itself upon the payer, unless it naturally falls on the person behind him. A tax on a house naturally falls on the landlord, as every land-valuer will tell you, and this universal payment by the landlord would speedily confirm the natural tendency, and leave the shoulders of the Occupier unburdened.

These three measures, the Equalization of Rating in all large Towns,—a Rate in Aid from the unrated portions of Schedules D and E, and the separation of the Landlords' and Tenants' proportion of the Rates,—would relieve very considerably the pressure of the Rates on the Working Classes, and to some extent the excessive amount of the Rates on the Landowners.

Such appear to be the measures desirable, and at a favourable moment they may be attainable by legislation. It is important that there should be some direct tax upon the Working Classes, not of an onerous character, but just sufficient to keep alive a sense of responsibility, and an interest in the national finances. Indirect Taxes have not this merit. Financial Reformers themselves have supported such a tax, both for these reasons, and also

Summary and Conclusion. 157

because they consider such Taxation more healthy and less expensive than indirect Taxes, for which it might ultimately be substituted.

The imposition of a direct Tax upon the Working Classes is always very difficult. But here it would be a substitute for a direct Tax of a much more serious nature, the occupier's Poor Rate, and would be welcomed as a relief; being small and certain in amount, and regular in time of payment: instead of large, uncertain, and irregular. If compounding is generally substituted for direct payment of Rates, the opportunity is not likely to recur.

The measures recommended are therefore as follows:—

I. The early repeal of the Taxes on Locomotion, Fire Insurance, and Corn, amounting to £2,620,000.

II. As regards Alcoholic drinks.
    1. The reform of the Licensing system, with the view of diminishing the amount of drinking.
    2. The improvement of the Malt Tax.
    3. Stringent measures against adulteration.

III. As regards Tea and Coffee, the repeal of the License system.

158 *Summary and Conclusion.*

CHAP. XXI.

IV. As regards Local Rates.
   1. Equalization of Rating in the Metropolis and large towns.
   2. A Rate in aid of the Poor Rate from the unrated portions of the Schedules D and E of the Income Tax.
   3. The division into separate taxes of the Landlords' and Tenants' portions of the Rates.

The results of such changes would be to remedy in some measure the extreme inequalities of some of the Taxes pressing upon the Upper and Middle Classes, and to lessen the Taxation of the Working Classes by the diminution of their Alcoholic expenditure and their Rates.

Let us consider for a moment in a more popular way the system of Taxation under which we live.

General view of Taxation.

The man of fortune, with a fine estate, and the accumulations of a prudent ancestor, has to pay to the State a heavy assessment upon its total value before he can enter on his inheritance. He pays taxes on his rents and dividends as often as he receives them. He pays them on his country seat and park, and on his more costly town mansion. He pays, though very lightly, at his breakfast table in the morning; if he goes out hunting, he pays upon his horse and hounds; if he shoots, he pays upon his gamekeepers and dogs, and for his own licence to sport; and he pays on his flask at the covert side, and on the cigar which circles its smoke into the air. If his wife drives out, he pays upon the coachman, the horses, the carriage, the armorial bearings. If he gives a dinner party, he pays upon the plate, upon the wine, and upon the butler and footman behind his chair. He pays a tax on the insurance of his house; he pays if he goes to law, and if he adds to his estate he pays still more.

The tradesman standing behind his counter pays upon his house and shop; and upon the food of his household; he pays upon his licences and insurances; he pays upon the legacy to his wife, and upon the house or field which his father has left; and he pays by small driblets in receipts and cheques. He struggles in vain in Vestry or Corporation against the continual growth of parish rates.

The workman pays only on his cottage and a few articles of consumption, but with the most temperate and careful habits he finds it hard to make both ends meet. He pays on his tea or coffee and sugar in the morning, on the tea that his wife and children drink at noon, and which he himself takes cold in a bottle to his work; and that they all drink together for their evening meal. He pays on the pipe that he smokes in walking home or by his fireside; and

CHAP. XXI.

he pays on his occasional glass of spirits and water and his daily glass of beer. The payments for these articles are far heavier on his income than on that of any other class.

But this is the brighter side of the picture, with clean homes, and school-going children, though sometimes hard pressed by toil or misfortune. Although there are local or peculiar cases of hardship, the system of taxation does not, as a whole, bear unjustly on temperate men. But there is also a dark side to the picture, where the gin-palace allures its throng of monomaniacs. The Custom-house officer takes toll at the door. The Excise-officer stands beside the till, and seizes nearly half the price of every glass that is poured. Emaciated and in rags, the drunkard puts down the wages that should have supported his children, calling for glass after glass until his earnings are exhausted, and then staggers off to a poverty-stricken home to wreak his madness upon his wife. Thousands, and tens of thousands, are mere funnels for drink, and divide all the sweat of their brow between the distiller and the State. Out of their folly the nation draws more than six millions of money, a twelfth of her whole Revenue; sufficient to support half her Navy, nearly sufficient to feed her destitute Poor. Such a source of

Summary and Conclusion.

Revenue is necessary, as a means of prevention. But we ought to be on our guard against the temptation of conniving at the vice for the sake of sharing the gain. We ought to take every opportunity of lessening drunkenness, even at the cost of diminishing our Revenue.

I conclude with a remark on the method of inquiry and the object of this work.

Taxpayers have a tendency to narrow their view to one or two particular imposts, and to draw inferences from them alone, ignoring all Taxes besides. Landowners and Farmers meet to complain of the local Rates upon Land, and demand their equalization over all kinds of property. Holders of Personalty look only at the probate and legacy duties, and on that ground complain that the land is unduly exempted from Taxation. A large school of economists concentrate their attention upon the Income Tax, and persuade themselves that Industrial Incomes are tyrannically overtaxed, because Schedule D makes no allowance for precariousness. The advocates of the Working Classes see nothing but their heavy Taxes on consumption, and treat as nothing the Taxes on property. I have endeavoured in these pages to point out to all these interests the importance of the rule, "LOOK AT TAXATION AS A WHOLE." Let them add up

Chap. XXI.

Taxation should be considered as a whole.

CHAP. XXI.

the different Taxes affecting each class of income, before complaining of "onerous inequality" as regards any one of them. Let them observe the Local Rates weighing heavily on the Land; the Probate and Legacy duties on Personalty; the Taxes on Consumption upon Working men; and the many exemptions of Industrial Incomes. It is only after considering all these that they can be in a position to pronounce a just opinion on remissions or additions to Taxation, and to do their part towards carrying out the principle so well expressed by Mr. Bright :—

House of Commons, July 21, 1859.

" The Taxes which now exist ought to be put on a satisfactory and honest footing, so that every man, and every description of property, may be called upon in its just proportion to support the burdens and necessities of the State."

APPENDIX I.

PROPERTY OF THE UNITED KINGDOM.

The Property of the United Kingdom is estimated as follows :—

1. REAL PROPERTY :—

	£
Lands, Houses, and Mines were assessed to Income Tax in 1866 at	132,000,000
Taken at 23 years' purchase, the average number for the total of the three kinds of property, the capitalized value is nearly	3,000,000,000
But from this must be deducted the *Leaseholds and Mortgages and Personalty in Mines*, estimated at one-third, or	1,000,000,000
Leaving the net capitalized value of the REAL PROPERTY OF THE UNITED KINGDOM . .	2,000,000,000

2. PERSONAL PROPERTY :—

(a) Mortgages, Leaseholds, &c., as above . . . 1,000,000,000

	Annual Value, Income Tax, 1865. £
(b) *Railways, Gas, and Canals* . .	23,000,000
Public Dividends on British, Colonial, and Foreign Funds, Schedule C.	34,000,000
Public Companies	12,000,000
	£69,000,000

Capitalized at 25 years' purchase these amount to £1,700,000,000

Brought forward . . .		£2,700,000,000

(c) Capital estimated to be employed in—
Capital

Farming, for £50,000,000 Rental under Schedule A. £300,000,000		
Their Animals alone are worth £170,000,000.)		
Trades and Professions, for £100,000,000 profit under Schedule D.	500,000,000	
Classes below the Income Tax .	200,000,000	
Dead Capital (Furniture, &c.) .	300,000,000	
		1,300,000,000
Total Personal Property		4,000,000,000
TOTAL REAL AND PERSONAL PROPERTY (*including the National Debt*)		£6,000,000,000

The above is based on the Income Tax, except as to Incomes below £100 and as to Furniture.

Personalty has often been estimated from the Probate Duties which are paid by Property passing under Wills or Intestacies, amounting, in 1867, to £1,770,000, which at 2 per cent. average Duty represents £88,000,000 of Property passing under Probate in that year.

Taking the Inland Revenue calculation of an average cycle of 30 years for each devolution of Property, we obtain the Total Personalty subject to Probate Duty as £2,640,000,000.

This leaves, out of the £4,000,000,000 above mentioned, £1,360,000,000 for the Personalty in Settlement, or below Probate Duties, or which evades them.

APPENDIX II.

UPPER AND MIDDLE CLASSES.

1.—Establishments and Consumption.

The following details have been given me by the kindness of a friend to show the Household Expenditure on Large Incomes:—

The Estate represents a clear rental of £6,000 a year.

Family—
- Masters 4
- Men Servants and Coachman in the house . 5
- Women Servants 12
-   21

Besides two men in the stables not having food in the house.

Articles.	Consumption.		Total Duty.
	Total.	Per Head.	£ s. d.
Tea	lbs. 230	lbs. 11	5 15 0
Coffee . . .	180	8¼	2 5 0
Sugar . . .	2,051	98	8 11 0
Wine . 166 galls.	bottles. 995	galls. 8	16 12 0
Beer	galls. 2,200	105	18 6 8
Spirits . . .	51	2½	17 17 0
			£69 6 8

The establishment is carefully managed, with a good deal of family reception and hospitality.

The Spirits and Soda-water are stated to be considerably in excess of the average, and the Wine deficient.

11,150 persons dined in the house during the year, of whom rather more than one-fourth were Visitors.

Over the whole of the estate the Land Tax is from 7 to 8 per cent. on the gross Rental.

The Insurance on the house is £58 a year, of which £23 is duty.

2.—CONSUMPTION OF WINES AND SPIRITS.

The following Table has been furnished to me by an eminent firm of Wine Merchants in London, as giving an approximate idea, from their experience, of the consumption of Wine and Spirits in the Upper and Middle Classes.

The Wine Duty is taken at an average of 2s. per gallon or 4s. per dozen (a dozen containing two gallons); and the Spirit Duty at 9s. per gallon, allowing for the Spirits being ordinarily sold at 10 per cent. below proof.

The average price of good-class Wine may be taken at 40s. per dozen, from the large quantity of claret that has come into consumption since 1860, and the greater competition. Before the French treaty it was considerably higher. Persons with large incomes buy higher priced Wines, and their bills show a higher average, than the smaller incomes.

The average of all the Wine imported, including the large quantities of low-class wines, is stated to be only 30s. per dozen.

The average price of Spirits consumed by the Upper and Middle Classes may be taken at 24s. per gallon or half dozen.

UPPER AND MIDDLE CLASSES.
Estimated Average Consumption of Wine and Spirits.

Income per Annum.	Consumption per Family.		Duty.	
	Wine.	Spirits.	Wine. Average 4s. per doz.	Spirits. Average 9s. per gal.
£	Dozen.	Gallons.	£ s. d.	£ s. d.
200	2	1	0 8 0	0 9 0
300	4	1	0 16 0	0 9 0
500	8	2	1 12 0	0 18 0
800	20	4	4 0 0	1 16 0
1,000	30	6	6 0 0	2 14 0
2,000	50	8	10 0 0	3 12 0
6,000	150	12	30 0 0	5 8 0
10,000	200	16	40 0 0	6 15 0

The Table shows an average expenditure on Wines and Spirits of about 5 per cent. on incomes above £500 a year; and that the Duties are about 10s. per cent. on the same incomes.

APPENDIX III.

TAXATION OF THE MANUAL LABOUR CLASSES.

The Returns which follow were obtained on the annexed Form, which was very kindly filled up, from personal inquiry of the families, by Clergymen, Vestry Clerks, Schoolmasters, and others having influence with the Working Classes, and in some instances by the Workmen themselves. When the Return was received, with the quantities properly entered, they were checked to detect inaccuracies, and the Taxation calculated in the margin. Returns from the same place were then arranged together and averaged. To those who can draw inferences from figures, the local groups will be interesting.

Table 1 contains two groups with high wages, where rent, tobacco, beer, and spirits are on a larger scale; and two others with lower wages, and economy in those items.

Table 2 shows the large Expenditure in tea, coffee, sugar, tobacco, and beer, which is common at Sheffield; and also common, with a considerable consumption of spirits in addition, further North, near Carlisle.

The lower scale of consumption near Wakefield, and still lower in the Hampshire Borough, should be noticed.

Table 3 gives the highest scale of agricultural Expenditure, in the manufacturing district near Sheffield; the next in Essex; the third in Hampshire; and the lowest of all, furnished by Canon Girdlestone, near Tiverton, where tea, sugar, and tobacco sink to their lowest point, and the wages are only £28 12s. per family.

FORM OF RETURN.

WORKING CLASSES.

*Number of Family*_____

	Amount per Year. £	REMARKS.
EARNINGS—		
Father _____ per Week, or . .	_____	
1 Mother _____ do. or . .	_____	
Children _____ do. or . .	_____	
Total Earnings . . . . £	_____	

	Shillings.	
Rent _____ per Week, or	_____	
Rates _____ in the £1, or	_____	
[If paid by Landlord, say so, but still give how much in the £1.]		

No. of lbs. or galls.	Quantity per year. lbs.
Tea _____ lbs. per week, or per year	_____
Coffee _____ lbs. do. or per year	_____
Sugar _____ lbs. do. or per year	_____
Tobacco _____ oz. per week, or per year	_____

	Gallons.
Beer _____ qts. or pots per week, or per year (4 to a gallon).	_____
Spirits _____ quarterns per week, or per year (32 to a gallon).	_____

APPENDIX III.

TAXATION OF THE MANUAL LABOUR CLASSES.
TABLE 1.—LONDON WORKMEN.

	Average of Fifteen Families of Journeyman Printers in Westminster.		Family, a Carpenter's at Clapham.		Average of Six Families, of an Engine Driver, Cabinet Maker, Shoemaker, &c., in Bethnal Green and Whitechapel, East London.		A Workman's Family at Hampstead.	
	Average per Family.	Taxes per Family.	Average per Family.	Taxes per Family.	Average per Family.	Taxes per Family.	Average per Family.	Taxes per Family.
Number per Family . . .	4½	—	4	—	6	—	6	—
	£ s. d.	£ s. d.	£ s. d.	£ s. d.	£ s. d.	£ s. d.	£ s. d.	£ s. d.
Earnings—Father . . .	92 0 0	—	78 0 0	—	49 10 0	—	54 0 0	—
Mother . . .	—	—	—	—	—	—	—	—
Children	—	—	20 16 —	—	4 0 0	—	—	—
Total Income	£92 0 0	—	£98 16 0	—	£53 10 0	—	£54 0 0	—
Rent (including Rates) . . .	25 0 0	—	16 18 0	—	13 17 4	—	11 14 0	—
Rates (paid by the Landlord) .	6 12 0	3 6 0	1 18 8	0 19 4	4 6 0	2 3 0	2 16 6	1 8 3
Tenant's half of Rate . .	—	—	—	—	—	—	—	—
Consumption of—	lbs.		lbs.		lbs.		lbs.	
Corn	21	0 2 3	13	0 2 6	19	0 3 6	26	0 3 0
Tea	21	0 10 6	13	0 6 6	5¼	0 9 1	—	—
Coffee	151	0 5 3	156	0 3 3	147	0 12 4	104	0 13 0
Sugar	6½	0 12 7	13	0 13 3	63	1 1 3	—	—
Tobacco	galls.	1 1 0	galls.	2 2 3	galls.	1 1 8	galls.	0 8 8
Beer	105	0 17 6	182	1 10 4	35	0 5 10	50	0 8 4
Spirits	2	0 15 6	1½	0 11 6	1	0 7 6	2	0 15 9
Net Taxation . .	. . .	£7 10 7	. . .	£6 8 2	. . .	£5 4 1	. . .	£3 16 9

APPENDIX III.

TABLE 2.—TOWN WORKMEN.

	Two Families of a Steel-worker and a Cutler at Sheffield, Yorkshire.		Six Families of Joiner, Mason, two Labourers, Shoemaker, and Tailor, at Abbey Town, near Carlisle, Cumberland.		Three Families, an Iron Labourer, a Forge Labourer, and a Fitter, at Wakefield, Yorkshire.		Two Families of Town Labourers at Christchurch, Hampshire.	
	Average per Family.	Taxes per Family.	Average per Family.	Taxes per Family.	Average per Family.	Taxes per Family.	Average per Family.	Taxes per Family.
Number per Family	5	—	5	—	7	—	5¼	—
Earnings—Father	£ s. d. 62 5 0	£ s. d. —	£ s. d. 47 0 0	£ s. d. —	£ s. d. 54 10 0	£ s. d. —	£ s. d. 32 10 0	£ s. d. —
Mother	—	—	6 10 0	—	—	—	2 10 0	—
Children	—	—	3 10 0	—	9 10 0	—	12 0 0	—
TOTAL INCOME	£62 5 0	—	£57 0 0	—	£64 0 0	—	£47 0 0	—
Rent	8 1 0	—	5 0 0	—	5 5 0	—	7 0 0	—
Rates: Tenant's half of Rates	3 0 0	1 10 0	0 10 0	0 5 0	1 0 0	0 10 0	0 11 0	0 5 6
Consumption of—	lbs.		lbs.		lbs.		lbs.	
Corn	32½	0 2 6	26	0 2 6	18	0 3 8	11½	0 2 9
Tea	39	0 16 4	50	0 13 0	9	0 9 3	—	0 2 5
Coffee	182	0 9 9	120	0 12 6	63	0 2 3	39	0 3 3
Sugar	14¾	0 15 2	6¼	0 10 0	6	0 5 4	6¼	0 1 2
Tobacco		2 7 0		1 1 0		0 19 6		0 4 4
	galls.		galls.		galls.		galls.	
Beer	156	1 6 0	150	1 5 0	76	0 16 8	26	—
Spirits	—	—	5	1 18 6	1	0 7 6	—	—
NET TAXATION	...	£7 7 0	...	£6 7 6	...	£3 14 2	...	£2 2 9

The Tobacco and Beer are large in the first two averages.

APPENDIX III.

TABLE 3.—AGRICULTURAL LABOURERS.

	Five Families, two near Sheffield and three near Wakefield, Yorkshire.		Two Families near Maldon, Essex.		Three Families near Christchurch, Hampshire.		Three Families near Tiverton, Devon.	
	Average per Family.	Taxes per Family.	Average per Family.	Taxes per Family.	Average per Family.	Taxes per Family.	Average per Family.	Taxes per Family.
Number in Family	6	—	5¼	—	5¾	—	5½	—
	£ s. d.	£ s. d.	£ s. d.	£ s. d.	£ s. d.	£ s. d.	£ s. d.	£ s. d.
Earnings—Father	39 0 0	—	45 10 0	—	32 0 0	—	22 10 0	—
Mother	3 12 0	—	—	—	4 0 0	—	1 15 0	—
Children	5 8 0	—	0 13 0	—	—	—	4 7 0	—
TOTAL INCOME	£48 0 0	—	£46 3 0	—	£36 0 0	—	£28 12 0	—
Rent	4 5 0	—	5 19 2	—	4 0 0	—	3 3 0	—
Rates	0 11 6	0 5 9	0 12 7	0 6 3	0 6 0	0 3 0	0 7 0	0 3 6
Tenant's half of Rates								
Consumption of—	lbs.		lbs.		lbs.		lbs.	
Corn	—	—	—	—	—	—	—	—
Tea	19	0 3 3	9¾	0 2 9	13	0 2 6	6¾	0 2 8
Coffee	13	0 0 3	—	0 4 10	—	0 6 6	4	0 3 3
Sugar	90	0 0 7	130	0 10 10	52	0 4 4	8½	0 0 2
Tobacco	6	0 19 6	3¼	0 10 6	6¼	0 1 1	2¼	0 0 9
	galls.		galls.		galls.			
Beer	68	0 11 4	26	0 4 4	26	0 4 4	Cider drinkers.	0 0 7
Spirits	—		—		—			
NET TAXATION		£3 0 1		£1 19 6		£2 1 8		£0 17 4

Appendix III.

TABLE 4.—TEA AND SUGAR.

The following Table is summarized from returns which were obtained for me with a great deal of other valuable information by Mr. Stanfield, of Wakefield.

CONSUMPTION OF TEA AND SUGAR.
BY 28 FAMILIES OF WORKMEN AT WAKEFIELD, 1868.

Average Number per Family	$5\frac{1}{2}$

Average Consumption per Family—	Per Head. lbs.
Tea, 18 lbs. per annum, or per head	$3\frac{1}{4}$
Sugar, 212 lbs. per annum, or per head	$38\frac{1}{2}$

TABLE 5.

The following is a Return from a Yorkshire village, not included in the foregoing :—

A temperate Agricultural Labourer, who has a wife and four young children.

The Wife can earn 1s. a day and her food, when her sister can "mind" the children at home, and thus enable her to clean or wash at some other house.

The Husband is skilled and active, and earns his £12 or £14 in Harvest, and the rest of the year 15s. per week.

His *Rent* for Cottage is £4 5s. per annum, for which he pays, himself, the rates, 2s. 6d. in the £1, on £2 10s.

His Rent for a rood of Allotment Garden is 12s. per annum, the rates paid by the Landlord.

Of *Tea*, they have 2 oz. per week, or $6\frac{1}{2}$ lbs. a year.
Of *Coffee*, none.
Of *Sugar*, about 2 lbs. per week, or 104 lbs. a year.
Of *Tobacco*, not more than 1 oz. per week, or $3\frac{1}{4}$ lbs. a year.
Of *Beer*—10 thrashing days, 10 quarts.

Turnip-sowing,	2 pecks malt =	6 gallons beer.
Hay-time	2 pecks malt =	6 gallons beer.
Harvest	$\frac{1}{2}$ load malt =	18 gallons beer.

Rest of year, a pint a week, say altogether 35 gallons.
Spirits, scarce a quart in a year.

The total Taxes will, therefore, be £1 11s. 6d. on £50 Earnings, or little more than 3 per cent.

Appendix III. 173

TABLE 6.

The Returns which are summarised below, have been sent to me by Mr. Tait, of Wakefield, from his inquiries of patients at the Wakefield Dispensary. Mr. Tait's list contains no names, but gives the ages, and many interesting details, which are necessarily omitted in the Summary.

MEN (12 in number).

Ten of temperate habits gave the following averages:—
  Tea, one and a half times per day by all.
  Coffee, only once a day by six.
  Tobacco, 1¼ oz. per week, average of nine.
  Beer, 2 pints a day, average of seven.
  Spirits, none.

Two intemperate:—
  Tea, none.
  Coffee, none.
  Tobacco, 1 oz. and 4 ozs. per week.
  Beer, 8 pints per day ordinary consumption, 15 to 20 pints as an excess. Used to be intoxicated three times a week.
  Spirits, none.

WOMEN (38 in number).

One, aged 63, nothing but milk.
Ten, *Tea* only, average three times a day.
  Tobacco, none.
  Beer, none.
Ten, *Tea*, average 2½ times a day.
  Tobacco, average ¼ oz. per week.
  Beer, none.
Seventeen, *Tea*, average twice a day.
  Tobacco, none.
  Beer, average ½ pint a day.
  Only three drink Coffee.
  None drink Spirits.
Thus 25 per cent. drink only Tea.
  25 per cent. take Tea, and smoke.
  50 per cent. drink Tea and Beer.
The notes that Tea is taken very strong and hot, are frequent.
One female, aged 36, takes Tea seven times daily.
Tea dust, at 10*d*. to 1*s*. 2*d*. per lb., was most commonly used.
The quantity of Tea used is stated as a quarter of a pound per week for the family for each daily tea-drinking. I should think that one-sixth of a pound would be a nearer average where Tea is taken more than once.

APPENDIX IV.

COMPARATIVE TOTAL TAXATION.

The following Tables give in detail the Taxes attributed to each Class.

The annexed explanations of the method of division are necessary in addition to the proportions given in the Tables themselves.

The Taxes on *Professions and Ordinary Trades* are divided, one-half to Income, and one-quarter to Expenditure of Upper and Middle Classes, one-quarter to Working Classes.

The *Mercantile Taxes*, one-quarter to Income, and one-quarter to Expenditure of Upper and Middle Classes, one-half to Working Classes.

The *Conveyance and Intercourse Taxes*, £500,000 to Income, and £1,560,000 to Expenditure of Upper and Middle Classes, £307,000 to Working Classes; since the Railway Taxes and Post Office surplus are almost exclusively borne by the Upper and Middle Classes.

The *Licenses* are calculated with the Wine, Beer, Spirits, and Tobacco.

The *Rates* are divided £12,500,000 to Income of Upper and Middle Classes (being £6,500,000 for Land, Railways, &c., and £6,000,000, the Landlords' half of Upper and Middle and Lower Classes.)

£4,000,000 as Tenant's half of Upper and Middle Classes.

£2,000,000 as Tenant's half of Working Classes.

Corn, Tea, Sugar, are divided by the rates per head given in Chapter xiii., adding in the case of Sugar a similar proportion of the quantity used by brewers and confectioners.

Alcohol.—*Temperate Consumption* on the scale given in page 91.

Intemperate Consumption.—The remainder divided rather less than one-fourth to Upper and Middle, and more than three-fourths to Working Classes.

Tobacco.—Upper and Middle Classes 2lbs. per head. Working Classes 1½lb per head.

Appendix IV.

TABLE 1.—TAXATION OF THE UPPER AND MIDDLE CLASSES.

ITEMS.	Proportion of Tax.	Amount.	Total.
NUMBER for whom they pay Taxes (including Servants)	—	—	8,000,000
INCOME	—	—	£490,000,000
TAXATION:			
ON INCOME—		£	£
Income Tax	all	6,177,000	
Land Tax	all	1,093,000	
Probate, Legacy, and Succession Duties	all	4,656,000	
Stamps and Law Funds	all	1,820,000	
On Professions, Trades, and Intercourse—			13,746,000
Professions and ordinary Trades	½	288,000	
Mercantile	¼	486,000	
Conveyance, &c.	part	500,000	
Local Taxes—			1,274,000
Rates on Land, Railways, &c. and Landlords' half	—	12,500,000	
EXPENDITURE:			12,500,000
I. Houses and Establishments—			
Rates, Tenants' half	—	4,000,000	
Tolls	all	1,225,000	
Assessed Taxes	all	2,360,000	
Racehorses, Plate, Game, Dogs	all	590,000	
Fire Insurance	part	674,000	
Professions and ordinary Trades	½	144,000	
Mercantile	¼	487,000	
Conveyance	part	1,560,000	
II. Corn, Tea, &c.—			11,040,000
Corn	½	200,000	
Tea (5½ lbs. per head)	½	1,127,000	
Sugar (50 lbs. per head)	½	2,260,000	
Coffee and Fruits	—	697,000	
III. Tobacco & Alcohol— (Temperate Consumption.)			4,284,000
Wine and Licenses	all	1,800,000	
Beer and Licenses	½	2,300,000	
Spirits and Licenses	½	2,625,000	
Tobacco and Licenses	¾	2,531,000	
			9,056,000
Total	—	—	£51,900,000
Beer and Spirits—Excessive or Intemperate Consumption			2,100,000
GRAND TOTAL			£54,000,000

TABLE 2.—TAXATION OF THE MANUAL LABOUR CLASSES.

ITEMS.	Proportion of Tax.	Amount.	Total.
NUMBER, exclusive of house servants	—	—	22,000,000
INCOME	—	—	£325,000,000
TAXATION:		£	£
I. Rates	—	2,000,000	
Trades	¼	144,000	
Mercantile	½	975,000	
Conveyance and Intercourse . . .	part	307,000	
			3,426,000
II. *Corn, Tea, &c.*—			
Corn	¾	670,000	
Tea (3 lbs. per head).	⅘	1,700,000	
Sugar (25 lbs. per head)	⅝	3,386,000	
Coffee and Fruits .	—	300,000	
			6,056,000
III. *Alcohol and Tobacco*—			
Beer (temperate consumption) . . .	—	2,570,000	
Spirits (ditto) . . .	—	6,300,000	
Tobacco	⅜	4,090,000	
			13,140,000
Total . .	—	—	£22,622,000
Intemperate or Excessive Consumption of Alcohol.	—	—	6,490,000
GRAND TOTAL . .	—	—	£29,112,000

APPENDIX V.

The two following Tables give the value of Tea, Coffee and Sugar; and of Wine, Beer, and Spirits in their stages from the bonded Warehouses, or the Brewer or Distiller, to the Public.

The prices given are those at respectable shops and for quantities not less than 1 lb., 1 bottle, or 1 gallon, and do not include the high prices for small quantities charged by the petty retail trade.

TABLE I.

TEA, COFFEE, AND SUGAR.

This Table has been made up by information derived mainly from Messrs. Law, the large Tea and Coffee Dealers of 544, New Oxford Street, and has been checked by information derived from other sources.

Coffee and Chicory.—The above table gives the net quantity, after deducting 20 lbs. per cwt. for the loss in roasting Coffee and 28 lbs. per cwt. for the similar loss in roasting Chicory. The net amounts of Coffee and Chicory and their values are thrown together, and the average taken on the total. The Duty (being the amount paid on the gross quantity before loss) comes to $3\frac{3}{4}d$. on the net quantity after roasting.

Sugar.—The quantity taken—1,150,000,000 lbs.—is the net quantity after deducting 200,000,000 lbs. for Brewers, Confectioners, and waste in refining.

The Value, before paying Duty, of Tea, Coffee, and Sugar, is taken approximately from the Statistical Abstract, p. 31.

TABLE II.

WINE, BEER, AND SPIRITS.

This table has been made up (except as to Beer) from information derived from two eminent firms of Wine Merchants, Messrs. Basil Woodd and Sons, and Messrs. Gorman and Co.

Beer.—The amount of Beer is taken at an average of 18 gallons per bushel of Malt. The Duty and Licenses make up together $2d.$ per gallon.

The calculation is worked out from the figures given in the evidence of Mr. W. Carling, before the Malt-Tax Committee 1867, Q. 349 to 366.

British Spirits.—British Spirits are diluted to the extent of 25 per cent. below proof. Mr. McLaren, in his evidence before the Sale of Liquors Committee, stated that this was the regular rule of Spirit sellers; and it is, no doubt, sometimes largely exceeded. The quantity thus produced is 28,800,000 gallons, and this is treated through the rest of the Table as the actual amount sold to the public. The Duty on a gallon of Spirits rather more than 25 per cent. below proof would be about 7s. 5d. The amount received for Spirit Licenses comes to an average of 4d. per gallon of diluted Spirit, making a total for Duty and Licenses of 7s. 9d.

Foreign and Colonial Spirits.—The per centage of dilution here is not so large on brandy, but is large on rum, and may be taken, on the whole, at 15 per cent. making 9,500,000 gallons of diluted spirit. The Duty and Licenses may be taken, in the same manner, at 9s. 2d. per gallon.

The value before paying Duty of the Wine, and Foreign and Colonial Spirits, is calculated on the prices given in the Statistical Abstract, p. 31.

III.

TOBACCO.

It is not possible to give a correct Table of Tobacco, since the proportion sold as Cigars is not known.

Supposing one-sixth to be sold in that form and five-sixths as Tobacco, the total value as sold to the Public is estimated at £20,000,000.

IV.

PROFITS.

The sellers' Profits in all the Tables include interest on Capital, and all Trade expenses, which form a very considerable deduction from the gross Profit.

For instance, in the higher Wine Trade the interest beyond what can be charged to the customer on the wines and brandies kept some years reduces very considerably the amount of Profits.

APPENDIX V.

TABLE 1.—VALUE OF TEA, COFFEE, AND SUGAR SOLD TO PRIVATE CONSUMERS, 1867.

	Tea.	Coffee and Chicory.	Sugar.	Total.
1. *Quantity retained for Home Consumption*	lbs. 111,000,000	Coffee, lbs. 25,600,000 Chicory, lbs. 7,125,000 32,725,000	lbs. 1,150,000,000	lbs. 1,293,725,000
2. *Value before paying Duty "Short price"—*				
Per lb.	1s. 7d.	8d.	2½d.	
Total	£8,788,000	£1,090,000	£12,000,000	£21,878,000
Per cent. on selling value	59 per cent.	47 per cent.	55¼ per cent.	56 per cent.
3. *Duty—*				
Per lb.	6d.	3¾d.	1d.	
Total	£2,775,000	£512,000	£4,800,000	£8,087,000
Per cent. on selling value	19 per cent	22 per cent.	22⅔ per cent.	21 per cent
4. *Refining or Roasting—*				
Per lb.	—	1¼d.	¼d.	
Total	—	£170,000	£2,400,000	£2,570,000
Per cent on selling value	—	7 per cent	11 per cent.	7 per cent.
5. *Wholesale and Retail Traders' Profit, Trade Expenses, and Interest on Capital—*				
Per lb.	7d.	4d.	½d.	
Total	£3,237,000	£546,000	£2,400,000	£6,183,000
Per cent. on selling value	22 per cent.	24 per cent.	11 per cent	16 per cent.
6. *Selling Value—*				
Average per lb.	2s. 8d.	1s. 5d.	4½d.	
TOTAL	£14,800,000	£2,318,000	£21,600,000	£38,718,000

APPENDIX V.

Table 2.—Value of Wine, Beer, and Spirits, 1867.

	Wine.	Beer.	British Spirits.	Foreign and Colonial Spirits.	Total.
1. *Quantity retained for Home Consumption*	Gallons. 13,600,000	Malt Bushels. 47,000,000 Beer gallons. 850,000,000	Gallons proof. 21,600,000 as sold 28,800,000	Gallons proof. 8,300,000 as sold 9,500,000	Gallons. 901,900,000
2. *Value before paying Duty*— Per gallon . . . . Total . . . . Per cent. on selling value	6s. 3d. £4,250,000 42 per cent.	6½d. £23,020,000 54 per cent.	2s. 3d. £3,240,000 15 per cent.	3s. £1,420,000 14½ per cent.	£31,930,000 38 per cent.
3. *Duty and Licenses*— Per gallon sold . . Total . . . . Per cent. on selling value	2s. £1,360,000 13 per cent.	2d. £7,080,000 16 per cent.	7s. 9d. £11,160,000 52 per cent.	9s. 2d. £4,350,000 44½ per cent.	£23,950,000 28¼ per cent.
4. *Storage, Bottling, and Waste*— Per gallon . . . . Total . . . . Per cent. on selling value	2s. £1,360,000 13 per cent.	— —	— —	1s. 6d. £710,000 7½ per cent.	£2,070,000 2½ per cent.
5. *Sellers' Profits, Expenses, and Interest on Capital*— Per gallon . . . . Total . . . . Per cent. on selling value	4s. 9d. £3,230,000 32 per cent.	3½d. £12,400,000 30 per cent.	5s. 0d. £7,200,000 33 per cent.	6s. 10d. £3,250,000 33½ per cent.	£26,080,000 31 per cent.
Selling value per gallon . . .	15s.	1s.	15s.	20s. 6d.	—
Total Value . . .	£10,200,000	£42,500,000	£21,600,000	£9,730,000	£84,030,000

N.B.—The amounts are calculated on the number of gallons of *diluted* Spirits, not on proof gallons.

www.ingramcontent.com/pod-product-compliance
Lightning Source LLC
Chambersburg PA
CBHW032149160426
43197CB00008B/827

Moroccan Mystique

Tales from a Timeless Journey

by

William Keenan

Copyright © 2023 William Keenan – Travel Top 10

All rights reserved.

ISBN:979-8-218-13070-1

DEDICATION

This book is dedicated to Naima Belghiti and Abdesalam Ketami. Naima was our dear friend, business partner and window into the world of Moroccan mysticism. Abdesalam was our dear friend, Arabic teacher, and mentor of Sufi philosophy.

Naima and Abdesalam both generously opened the doors to their homes, hearts, and families. Although they have both passed away, their spirits remain guiding lights to international peace and understanding.

Travel – it leaves you speechless, then turns you into a storyteller.

- Ibn Battuta